Building the Possible Through Impossibilities

By Terry Bethea

Building the Possible Through Impossibilities
Copyright © 2015

Contact Info
Author: Bishop T.J. Bethea
New Gospel Missionary Baptist Church
P.O. Box 44004
Fayetteville, N.C. 28309
(910) 484-9008
E-mail: bishopbethea@gmail.com
churchadmin@newgospelmbc.org

Cover design: Anointed Fire™House
Publisher: Anointed Fire™ House
Publisher's Website: www.anointedfirehouse.com

All scriptures noted in this book were taken from the KJV or the NIV bible unless otherwise noted.

ALL RIGHTS RESERVED.
This book contains material protected under International and Federal Copyright Laws and Treaties. Any unauthorized reprint or use of this material is prohibited. No part of this book may be reproduced or transmitted in any form or by any means, electronic or mechanical, including photocopying, recording, or by any information storage and retrieval system without express written permission from the author / publisher.

You may NOT sell or redistribute this book!

ISBN-13: 978-0692428894 (Anointed Fire)

ISBN-10: 0692428895

Disclaimer: This book is designed to provide information and motivation to our readers. It is sold with the understanding that the publisher is not engaged to render any type of psychological, legal, or any other kind of professional advice. No warranties or guarantees are expressed or implied by the author, since every man has his own measure of faith. The individual author(s) shall not be liable for any physical, psychological, emotional, financial, or commercial damages, including; but not limited to, special, incidental, consequential or other damages. Our views and rights are the same: You are responsible for your own choices, actions, and results.

The stories in this book are fictional. Names, characters, businesses, places, events and incidents are either the products of the author's imagination or used in a fictitious manner. Any resemblance to actual persons, living or dead, or actual events is purely coincidental.

Acknowledgments

I would like to take this opportunity to acknowledge those who encouraged, inspired and motivated me to write this book and to those who stuck by me when the fire got hot. There are many people I can acknowledge, some who were supportive and some not so supportive.

I want to thank my mother Brenda A. Hodge for her love and making me the man I am today. Mother, I love you and I pray this book will make you proud of me.

To my grandparents Pastor Jesse (Goodtime) Brown and Deacon Warren Brown for teaching me true holiness and the value of living holy.

To my brother Matthew whose life ended too soon: Thank you for your determination and encouragement.

To my other siblings John, Cheryl, and LeAnn: I will always love you.

To the love of my life, my diva-lovely wife, Teasia O'Shell-Homer Bethea: Thank you for your love, support, and making each day better than the last. Thank you for walking with me through the struggles, trying times, sleepless nights and joyful days. Your love has made me a better man, and keeping you happy is my goal. I love you dearly.

To my children Katisha, Terry Jr., Latovia, Jimmy, Bianca, Sidney, Teiara, and DeAndre: I love all of you—Dad.

To New Gospel Missionary Baptist Church family: The house and family God has given me—thank you.

To the most important person who makes all of this possible: To my Lord and Savior Jesus Christ—the glory belongs to God.

Preface

This book was written as an inspiration to those of you who are determined to build a church building, a ministry, and more than anything, your faith. Nothing is too hard for God; I am a living witness to this. Whatever you set your mind to do, you can do it. The first step is to consult God and follow His lead.

Introduction

One of the greatest accomplishments a man can have is to win the soul of another man for the kingdom of heaven. We get so caught up in the world's idea of success that we often lose touch with the most important gift that God has given us, and that gift is love. Being chosen to lead the people of God is an honorable duty, but it can also be a challenging one because a minister's faith is always being stretched. After all, ministers of the gospel of Jesus Christ not only win souls for the kingdom, they help believers to do what they are designed to do: believe. How can one call himself or herself a believer if that person does not believe? The truth is, we all believe something, but a minister's job is to get people to believe God.

You've accepted the assignment on your life, and the first challenge you're faced with is almost always going to be lack of knowledge. Where do you start? How do you start a ministry? With all of the confusing doctrines and man-made traditions out today, it is easy to become overwhelmed and want to give up, but don't throw in the towel just yet.

In *Building the Possible Through Impossibilities*, I am going to share knowledge with you that's essential to building a successful and progressing ministry. In your attempts to build the vision God has given you, you will no longer have to sort through the many ungodly traditions that have crept into the church. This wealth of information will build your knowledge, strengthen your faith, and sharpen your understanding.

Table of Contents

Acknowledgments..V

Preface...VII

Introduction...IX

   My Testimony..1

   Facing the Impossible..13

   Self Discovery..31

   The Faith to Move Mountains...............................41

   A Prophet Without Honor..57

   The Truth About 501c3..77

   Life and Challenges of a Chosen Person....85

   The Truth About Denominations.....................103

   Five Fold Ministry Offices..119

   The Office of the Bishop...137

   Starting a Ministry...145

   Building a Ministry 163

   Faith Versus Goliath...181

My Testimony

When God starts to move and position you, things next to or around you become re-positioned. When God moves you, things that are connected to you must move. In Genesis 28:13, Jacob called Joseph in so he could bless him. When you have purpose in your life, the most promising thing that can be rewarded to you is someone blessing you for your assignment. Over the course of my life, I have heard people say, "You are blessed" and "God is going to bless you." Of course, I have accepted these statements, but when the challenges of life comes my way and I don't feel blessed, I am reminded that being chosen doesn't always look promising or good. After all, most of us don't look like what we've been through.

Just because you are chosen doesn't mean

My Testimony

you are on the top of the heap; the heap may be on top of you. If you are going to build, you must first look at yourself and make sure you are able to handle the construction, and of course, I am referring to physical construction. Physical construction is being able to take the pressures that come with life and still keep standing. Without this construction, we would be houses without foundations; we'd be unstable and low.

Isaiah 64:6 (KJV): But we are all as an unclean thing and all our righteousnesses are as filthy rags; and we are do fade as a leaf and our iniquities, like the wind, have taken away.

Luke 14:28 (KJV): For which of you, intending to build a tower, sitteth not down first, and counteth the cost, whether he have sufficient to finish it?

If you are like myself, you are not a celebrity. You don't have high paying speaking engagements, a large budget, or million dollar tithe payers. Your church is not on one of the top Christian television stations, nor is it on any of the most talked about gospel radio stations.

My Testimony

You are simply waiting for your season. When God entrusts you to lead a handful of people, He is testing your measure of faith. We must remain appreciative and humble about our present state of affairs, otherwise, God can bring us down and humble us.
Luke 14:11 (KJV): For whosoever exalteth himself shall be abased; and he that humbleth himself shall be exalted.

When you are chosen by God, you must take care to not allow where you are today hinder where you're supposed to be tomorrow. The journey of a chosen vessel is not an easy path to walk because everyone's eyes will be on you, and everything you do will be scrutinized.

I thought I was only going to preach for a Sunday, but God had other plans. That Sunday was the longest Sunday of my preaching life because I am still here. I did not set out to build a church or a ministry. I had no idea that God was positioning me to do (in my mind) the impossible through impossibilities. We wandered in our personal deserts for

My Testimony

years, and I often joked that the Israelites had nothing on us. We wandered around for nine years, but if felt more like 99 years. We were a small church looking for a home, and I thought because I was God's chosen, it would be easy for me to put His people in a permanent home. I was wrong.

Romans 8:14 (KJV): For as many as are led by the Spirit of God, they are the sons of God.

We went from pillar to post, post to pillar, and then, back to where we started out. One Saturday morning, God led me to the land we are on now. I was driving when God spoke. He told me which roads I was to turn on as I approached those roads, and being obedient to the voice of God, I followed His directions. I turned onto a piece of land, and suddenly, it dawned on me that God had delivered me to our new church home. The "for sale" sign was hidden behind the tall grass. I was overwhelmed and my emotions got the best of me. God was in the plan. I immediately called the number on the sign, but to my disappointment, the price was too high for a

My Testimony

small congregation. Obviously, the price did not deter me, so I called the church's trustee and the financial secretary. We made arrangements to meet up and went to the local bank, hoping for good news. We went in full of enthusiasm and zeal. Nevertheless, we left the bank downhearted because the bank declined our offer. I did what I knew to do, and that was to go to the church and ask the members to help. We started a financial drive, but it was not a raffle, a cake sale, or anything like that. My motto was: *No chickens will die to pay for the church*; it will come from our small congregation and friends. The Nehemiah Fund was established and the members were to pledge a certain amount of money to help us reach our six month deadline. We reached our deadline in five months and raised the $25,000.00 that we need. We'd raised enough for the building, but we did not have enough to pay for the land, nevertheless, when you are chosen and your team is on one accord, God will move. God touched the heart of one of the deacons to get a loan for the money we needed, and he helped us to pay that loan

My Testimony

back. Needless to say, that deacon was blessed in business and other areas of his life for stepping out on faith for his church.

The next mountain we had to face was the owner of the land. He did not want to come down on the price of the land, nevertheless, we were determined to get it. God spoke and told me to present an offer, but he refused my offer. Not dismayed, I decided to try one more time. This time, I called his house and his wife answered the phone. We talked shortly, and she asked me, "If I can get my husband to agree to the price you offered, will you still get the land?," and of course, I agreed. She spoke with her husband, and he finally agreed to sell the land to us at a reasonable price, so we went to see our prospective attorneys to put the sale into motion.

The next mountain we came to was financing. No one wanted to finance us, so we put a sign up on the land that read: *The future home of New Gospel Missionary Baptist Church.* This sign stayed up for a year and six months. We

My Testimony

held services at the local hotel, and then, we shared a church for a while. After that, we were back to having services at the local hotel. We were God's people wandering in the wilderness. Nevertheless, the most extraordinary part of it all was, even though we held one service a week, we'd never lost a member. Instead, our membership continued to grow while we were in our wilderness experience.

The next installment God had in mind was wonderful. One evening, one of the deacons of the church came to my home and said, "Pastor please come take a ride with me." I thought he was taking me out to eat, but that was not the plan. The trip was pretty extensive and I didn't have a clue as to where we were going. He turned onto a parking lot and said, "Pastor, do you see that white building?" I looked at the building and it looked like a bomb had hit it. It was old and the paint was cracking —I laughed. He asked me to go inside and take a look, and after we went inside, he asked me what I thought of the building. "It's alright,"

My Testimony

I said, but in my mind, I was saying, "It's nothing to write home about." He told me that he'd received a call that day, and the caller asked him if he knew anyone who was in need of a church building, and he thought of me.

After we left the building, he drove me back to my house, and as we stood on my porch, I confessed to him that the church was not the two thousand seat sanctuary I was hoping for. It was at that moment that I heard God say, "You have to start somewhere." This was a humbling moment. It wasn't what I desired or dreamed of, but it was what God wanted for us at that time. You have to let God lead, because what you see as a dilapidated building, God sees your future.
James 4:10 (KJV): Humble yourselves in the sight of the Lord, and He shall lift you up.

With James 4:10 in mind, I started on a journey of self-discovery, faith walking, and humility. I did not know where the road was going to lead to, but I had to follow it. I am a soldier in the army of the Lord, and I had just received my marching orders. My assignment was placed before me, and I was ready to go.

Psalms 27:14 (KJV): Wait on the Lord: be of good courage, and he shall strengthen thine heart; wait, I say on the Lord .

I was concerned about the flock God placed in my care, when out of nowhere, a blessing came. A local company heard of what we were attempting to do and offered to help. The Lord heard the prayers and cries of His children in the wilderness. I could finally see the light at the end of the tunnel. Things were starting to move in the right direction. The financier was a Godsend; she made the necessary adjustments in the church's building. It was hard to get financing in what the world called a recession. She called everyday to reassure me that things were on track—then came another mountain to climb. The phone calls stopped coming, so I started calling the company that the financier worked for. At first, I couldn't reach anyone, but when I finally got through, I was saddened to hear that she was no longer employed with the company. My

My Testimony

heart sank, my spirit was hit hard, and my faith was again put to the test. I went back to the congregation and we continued with our pledge drive.

A few months passed and the Lord continued to give me strength and renew my faith. Every Sunday, the congregation would meet, and we praised God as if we were already in our new home. One Sunday, a prophetic spirit fell and God spoke to His people, reassuring them that He will answer their prayers. After that Sunday, we received a call and were informed that our paperwork was given to a financial representative who vowed to make sure we got the money we needed. Our faith began to work in our favor. The impossibilities became possibilities.

We started putting things into motion for the stages of building the church. The next obstacle came when we bought the building with the money we had. Now the land had to be prepared to receive the building. Once the land was prepared, the next step was to move

My Testimony

the building from its present location to its new location. At that moment, I felt relieved; my faith had held out. I thought back to the time when one of the deacons and I held sunrise service on the land. We read scriptures, sang songs and prayed. We wanted God to know that we appreciated everything He has done for us thus far, and that we were committed to making the building process a success.

We were on our way—the foundation for the building was laid, and the church was disassembled into three parts. Each part had to be loaded on the trucks and moved to the new location. I felt like a new father waiting for his child to be born. Finally, the three parts of the building arrived, and as we waited on the contractor to put the jigsaw puzzle together, we faced our greatest mountain—we ran out of money.

The point is we're in the building now. We've faced many mountains, but nothing has stopped us from receiving what God had for us. The purpose of this book is to encourage

My Testimony

those of you who are starting or running churches. You will succeed as long as you obey the Lord and follow the trail that He puts before you.

This book is a treasure trove of information, written to help encourage, educate, and teach you as you build the ministry God has given you to build. Be encouraged and know that God cannot and will not fail you. The struggle is never with Him.

Facing the Impossible

When you're looking to start a ministry, one thing you'll find is there are a lot of roadblocks on your path, and these roadblocks make your journey difficult. You may even come across some obstacles that appear to be impossible to get past. Nevertheless, there is nothing too hard for God, and the only thing that's impossible for God to do is lie.

We've all had our fair share of trials, tribulations, and obstacles, and over the courses of our lives, those challenges have transformed or deformed our faith. That's because we all have our own individual ways of facing opposition. Some of us react with our flesh first, and when we see that our flesh isn't getting us what we want, we start using scriptures, prayers, and fasting. Because of this, we tend to place labels on any and

Facing the Impossible

everything we can't seem to get past, and all too often, we label those things as impossible.

But what does the word "impossible" mean? According to reference.com, "impossible" is defined as:
- not possible; unable to be, exist, happen, etc.
- unable to be done, performed, effected, etc.
- an impossible assignment.
- incapable of being true, as a rumor.

As you see, one of the definitions is: *unable to be, exist, or happen.* What's amazing is God has given us (mankind) the ability to speak life or death, but we often use our authority the wrong way. We call things impossible that are possible through Christ Jesus, and we do this only when we don't recognize our rights or the authority that lives in us.

When God took Ezekiel up in the spirit, He wanted to demonstrate His power through Ezekiel. He took Ezekiel to a place where

Facing the Impossible

there was nothing but human skeletal remains. Now, it's amazing for us, as believers, to see a human who's been declared dead brought back to life, but imagine how breathtaking it was to see life given to skeletal remains. Ezekiel gives his account of this amazing phenomena in Ezekiel 37:1-3 (NIV), and it reads, "The hand of the Lord was on me, and he brought me out by the Spirit of the Lord and set me in the middle of a valley; it was full of bones. He led me back and forth among them, and I saw a great many bones on the floor of the valley, bones that were very dry. He asked me, "Son of man, can these bones live?" I said, "Sovereign Lord, you alone know."

One thing you'll notice about Ezekiel's account is he mentioned that the bones were very dry. Ezekiel's testimony not only demonstrated that the bones had no flesh on them, but they were dry bones, meaning, they'd been dead for a while. There was no sign of life left on those bodies, and that's why God chose them to show His power through. As you read on, another thing you'll notice is that God did not

Facing the Impossible

directly tell the bones to get up, but He instructed Ezekiel to speak His words over those bones.

Ezekiel 37:4-8: Then he said to me, "Prophesy to these bones and say to them, 'Dry bones, hear the word of the Lord! This is what the Sovereign Lord says to these bones: I will make breath enter you, and you will come to life. I will attach tendons to you and make flesh come upon you and cover you with skin; I will put breath in you, and you will come to life. Then you will know that I am the Lord.' "
So I prophesied as I was commanded. And as I was prophesying, there was a noise, a rattling sound, and the bones came together, bone to bone. I looked, and tendons and flesh appeared on them and skin covered them, but there was no breath in them.

Ezekiel had to do something that went beyond his realm of understanding, something that stood outside the natural realm of possibilities. He had to believe that the dry bones he was seeing could live. He then had to speak to those bones and tell them what God said He was about to do to them. Once Ezekiel obeyed God and spoke the words he was commanded to speak, those bones began to come together and flesh began to cover those bones. He mentioned that everything God had spoken began to take place the very moment he started to prophesy what the Almighty and Sovereign God had told him to say. Now, there are several points we should take from what we've read so far.

1. As I mentioned earlier, Ezekiel's natural understanding had to be breached. He was taken outside the realm of natural possibilities so that he could experience the power of God. If you recall, Ezekiel said that he was taken up by the Spirit of God. What does this mean? It means that God likes to demonstrate His power through His Spirit. Whenever we are in the natural realm, we tend to lean to our natural understanding, and this limits what God can do for us. Now, He is the God of possibilities, meaning, He can take what's impossible and make it possible, but in the realm of the

Facing the Impossible

earth, God moves through willing vessels. He does this because He created the earth for mankind, and He created mankind to till the earth. God gave mankind dominion over the earth, and He gave man will instead of instinct. The difference between will and instinct is a person with will won't default to a certain behavior because of what he is. A human being makes choices based on what's in his heart, whereas, a creature with instinct will always default back to their instinct, even though it can make choices.

God took Ezekiel up with His Spirit, which, in itself, would be considered impossible to our natural reasoning. From there, God demonstrated His ability to bring dead, dry bones back to life.

The Word tells us to lean not to our own understanding. Why is that? When we lean to our understandings, we limit ourselves to what we've seen and heard. When we lean to our own understandings, we limit ourselves to human capabilities, not understanding that we can do all things through Christ who strengthens us. This isn't just the possible things, but the bible tells us that we can do ALL things through Christ. Christ is the key Word in this sentence, for He is the living Word of God.

2. God had Ezekiel to speak to the bones. Again, we are in the natural realm of the earth, but God is a Spirit, so God does not violate what He has established in the realm of the earth. God made it illegal for a spirit to operate in the earth's realm. God uses willing vessels to carry out His plans for the earth. He wanted to use Ezekiel to speak to the skeletal remains, and when Ezekiel obeyed Him, the bones began to come together, and flesh began to cover those bones.

All too often, we get distracted by what we see, not understanding that God's Word is Spirit; they are life. When we speak God's Word, we are speaking life, and we are speaking prophetically. We have the God-given ability to change what's impossible to possible by simply believing God, obeying the Lord, and speaking His Word. Nevertheless, to do this, we have to come outside our natural reasoning, refuse to lean to our own understanding, and believe God to do greater than we can ever ask or think.

3. When Ezekiel spoke to the dry bones, the very first thing he told them to do was "hear the Word of the Lord". Ezekiel was acknowledging that the words he was about to speak were not his own. Those bones did not have to obey Ezekiel, but they had to obey the Word of God. How does this affect you and I? All too often, in ministry, we try to speak our own words, not understanding that there are certain things in the realm of the earth that we don't have dominion over. We have dominion over the fish in the sea, the birds in the sky, and every creature walking in the earth, but we do not have dominion over human life. We

Facing the Impossible

have the power of life and death in our tongues, but we don't have dominion over human life, since we are spirit creatures. The bones Ezekiel saw didn't have any life in them. The spirits of the people who once lived in those shattered bodies had already left the earth's realm, and Ezekiel did not have the ability or right to call them back into the earth outside of God's permission. That's why Saul went to the witch of Endor in his attempt to conjure up Samuel. He didn't have the ability to bring Samuel's spirit back into his body, so he attempted to conjure up Samuel's spirit without an earthly body, and this act in itself is spiritually illegal. Ezekiel's act was legal because he was obeying the Lord, and he told those bones to hear the Word of the Lord, and not himself. All too often, we speak out of our emotions, and we wonder why things don't come to pass in our lives and ministries. It's because there are somethings that do not have to obey you, but they have to obey the Word of the Lord. For example, the angels of God do not have to obey human beings; they obey the Word of God, so to get them to move on your behalf, you have to speak the Word.

4. Ezekiel spoke in authority and not religiously. Ezekiel told the bones, "You will come to life." He didn't ask the bones to live, nor did he hope the bones would come to life. Ezekiel spoke in authority and the bones lived. Religion has taught us to politely ask for things, and if they don't come to pass, to practice a bunch of religious rituals in our attempts to get heaven to loose whatever we've been asking for. But we were given dominion and authority in the earth, therefore, we call those things that be not as though they were. We have to identify what's dead around us, and then, speak life into it.

What's impossible to man is possible to God because He is the Creator of all things,

Facing the Impossible

including heaven and earth. There is nothing too hard for God, but mankind tends to limit God based on his own understanding. When we place limitations on God, we restrict Him from exercising His limitless power in our lives. The power of God is with and in Him, regardless of whether we believe Him or not, but when we doubt God, we are, in the same, denying Him permission to demonstrate His effective power in our lives.

When we were children, we were taught and matured in the things of the world. We were taught what man considered possible, and what man said was impossible. Our schools even tested us to make sure we'd retained the knowledge they'd given to us. We were oblivious to the spirit world, even though many of us went to church and heard about the realm of the spirit. We mastered what we could see, and we continued to be ignorant of what we could not see. We watched as other children were teased about their strange beliefs, and most of us made up our minds to just agree with the majority. We chose what was possible or impossible to us, and as we grew older, the list of things we considered impossible continued to grow. Before long, we'd developed our own identities based on our beliefs. We continued to befriend people who thought like ourselves, and we tried to live our lives in ways that would assure that we were accepted by the people we respected the most. Then, one day, we gave our lives to Christ, and the whole idea of being born again was incomprehensible to us. Sure, we'd gotten saved, and we'd been baptized, but we didn't understand the concept of being born again. So, most of us entered salvation with our old mindsets, and we tried to make our new lives work with the old mentalities we were still in submission to. Nevertheless, our lives began to crumble because we were reading a bible that told us that much of what we'd been taught by the school system was a lie. What we'd considered impossible for so long was actually possible through Christ Jesus, but we're human. Anytime something goes outside the realm of a human being's understanding, that human becomes frustrated, argumentative,

Facing the Impossible

and defensive. So, whenever someone tried to tell us that it was possible for God to change our situations, our loved ones, and our lives, we became angry with them. Why? Because they were trying to introduce something foreign to our minds. They were speaking spiritual things into natural understandings.

As we grew in the Word, our list of impossibilities grew shorter, and our perception of the world and all it had to offer was altered. As we matured in Christ, we watched as our lives were changed. Old friends left us because they could no longer relate to us. New friends came into our lives, only to leave us once they'd decided they could no longer relate to us. We'd even found ourselves being rejected by some of the leaders in the church we'd once looked up to. It was evident that we were growing in the things of the Lord, and we started getting a better understanding of the power of God. Nevertheless, we continued to limit God out of fear because there were still some things we couldn't imagine God bringing to pass in our lives. Maybe we were believing

Facing the Impossible

God for a new house, or maybe, we were believing Him for a new car. Some of us were believing God for Godly spouses, and when we didn't see those things come to pass, our list of impossibilities started growing again. Why was this? Because we were beginning to understand that we didn't know how God worked after all. We knew that He is God, and we'd heard that all things are possible to those who believe, so we tried to move God with our works. We sang, we danced, and we ministered to others, hoping that God would see our works and reward us accordingly. When our works didn't move God, we turned to religious prayers where we repetitiously prayed the same prayer with different words. When God didn't answer our prayers, our list of impossibilities got longer. We tried many things to move God because we did not understand God. We were looking at Him from a religious standpoint, so we tried to deal with Him religiously. After many failed attempts to move God on our behalf, many turned away from God, others got even more religious, and then, there were the few who continued to seek

Facing the Impossible

an intimate relationship with God. Those who turned away from the Lord decided that His existence was impossible or He was impossible to deal with. They then turned to the beliefs they believed were possible, things that made more sense to their natural understandings. Those who turned to religion credited Him for being a possible God, but they believed that they had to work harder, pray longer, and fast more to move Him. Of course, their lists of impossibilities continued to grow because they kept praying amiss and didn't see the fruit of their prayers being made manifest in their lives. Finally, those who sought an intimate relationship with the Father, not only found Him, but they began to uncover the mysteries of His ways. They came to understand that God wasn't moved by works, scriptures, or religious sentiments; God is moved by our faith and our faith is built upon our understanding of who God is. In other words, we have to know the Word to move the Word. Those who sought an intimate relationship with the Lord found that their lists of possibilities grew longer as their lists of

Facing the Impossible

impossibilities grew shorter. Ezekiel had to be developed, pressed, and tried to get to the level of faith he was in. In order for him to speak to the dry bones he saw, he had to first believe that he was hearing from God, and then, he had to believe that God could bring those bones to life.

What are you believing God for in your life and ministry? How do you face the impossible? To face the impossible, you have to have faith in God, and then, you have to believe that God can work thorough you. One of the greatest hindrances that ever hit the church is self condemnation. All too often, we see our own flaws and think that God can't or won't work through us because of our imperfections, not understanding that Christ took our sins upon Himself and gave us His righteousness. When we are saved, God doesn't see our imperfect selves, He sees Christ in us. He also sees our measures of faith because our faith or lack thereof allows or limits what God can do in our lives. It doesn't limit Him as God, but it limits what He can do for us, since our faith is the

Facing the Impossible

vehicle that allows Him to move in our lives. Doubt, on the other hand, is the roadblock that we put up before God, disallowing Him to move in certain areas of our lives, and of course, doubt is often formed because of fear or ignorance. Doubt is always the response to a doctrine, whether written or unwritten, that goes against the Word of God.

A lot of people are going to oppose you when you decide to launch the ministry God has given you to launch, or, if you're already running a ministry, the enemy will do everything within his power to get you to close that ministry. That's a given, but your faith or lack of faith will determine who gets the victory in your life. What appears to be impossible to you is nothing more than an opportunity for God to demonstrate His miraculous powers through you. It's an opportunity for God to take something that does not exist and breathe life into it. Everything in your life and ministry that appears impossible is nothing more than dry bones, but it's up to you whether you believe those dry bones can live.

Self Discovery

When we were children in the natural, we all struggled to find our own identities, and this wasn't easy to do in a world dominated by cliques, fads, and peer pressure. We wandered around trying to make a name for ourselves because we thought if we were largely accepted by our peers, we'd become the great men or women we believed ourselves to be. We wanted to be accepted, and as we got older, we learned some valuable lessons about life. We learned to stop impersonating the men and women we once looked up to and just be ourselves. We learned that regardless of how we looked, behaved, or sounded, we'd be accepted by some and rejected by others. Some of us learned to be okay with being our imperfect selves, while others continued to master the art of character impersonation.

Self Discovery

One day, we gave our lives to the Lord and thought we could bring all of what we'd learned in the world with us. We thought our street smarts would be beneficial to the church and to our ministries, but we were met with spiritual resistance. Everything in our lives seemed to wither away, and we questioned whether we were in the will of God or not. What we didn't know was that we were on one of the first journeys to having effective ministries. We were on the journey to self discovery.

A preacher or teacher who doesn't know his identity is still in the nest of building his ministry, but he hasn't learned to fly just yet. The problem these days is a lot of leaders try to take flight before they've gotten their wings. They are not allowing God to complete the work in them that He is doing, and most people who are anxious to launch their ministries are the same people who are being enticed by the riches of this world. They see leaders who've been through the refining process and have started enjoying some of their God-given inheritances, and they begin to covet the titles,

Self Discovery

ministries and lifestyles of those leaders. When they see what other leaders have, they lose focus on their own assignments and start focusing on what they believe to be the perks of ministry. This distraction causes so many leaders to leave the nest too early in search of riches, fame and glory, only to fall into one of the many snares set by the enemy. In their vain searches for glory, they have left the trail of self discovery, a path that's vital to being an effective minister.

As a minister of the gospel, you can expect to be tried, but when trials come your way, it's how you handle those trials that will determine whether you are elevated or not. Sometimes, we tend to have two faces when it comes to our walks with Christ. We tend to wear our Christian persona whenever our lives are running smoothly, but whenever we hit a few bumps in the road, our flesh shows up and brandishes its ugly fangs. This means that instead of allowing ourselves to be transformed into the men and women God has called us to be, we keep trying to hold on to the old

Self Discovery

creature that we were. God allows us to go through trials so that we can be developed, reformed, and transformed into His glorious image. We will suffer persecution and trials for His name's sake if we are truly ministers of the gospel of Jesus Christ.

Matthew 5:10-12 (NIV): Blessed are those who are persecuted because of righteousness, for theirs is the kingdom of heaven. Blessed are you when people insult you, persecute you and falsely say all kinds of evil against you because of me. Rejoice and be glad, because great is your reward in heaven, for in the same way they persecuted the prophets who were before you.

2 Timothy 3:12-13 (NIV): In fact, everyone who wants to live a godly life in Christ Jesus will be persecuted, while evildoers and impostors will go from bad to worse, deceiving and being deceived.

Romans 8:17 (NIV): Now if we are children, then we are heirs--heirs of God and co-heirs with Christ, if indeed we share in his sufferings in order that we may also share in his glory.

Self Discovery

Discovering your own identity is a process that should not be taken lightly. During this process, you will meet betrayal, persecution, and scandal, but these things don't come forth to kill you. They come to try and prove you. The enemy would love to use those weapons to bring you down and discredit your ministry, but God allows you to go through the storms so you can effectively counsel His people. Leaders who don't have testimonies aren't as effective or powerful as leaders who do. That's because your audience will be filled with people who have been through some of the worst storms known to man, as well as people who are still going through those storms. If you haven't been through the heartache, the fear, and the doubt they're going through, most of them won't be able to receive counsel from you. But when people know you've been through the fire that they're in, they become encouraged in the fire simply because they see that you've escaped without being burned. The point is the process isn't there to kill you; it's there to build you. You have to know who you are, but you won't know who you are until

Self Discovery

you've been tried. Anyone can say they are a prophet, apostle, evangelist, teacher or pastor, but once they've all been tried, there is a great falling away. It's the people who've been tried by fire and kept by grace who are left standing once the enemy rages up against them. That's because the God in them cannot be taken down, and as long as they are in Christ, they won't fall either.

Below, you will find five tips to discovering yourself. These tips will help you as you start, launch, and build the ministry God has given you.

1. **Know who you are.** The key to knowing who you are is learning to identify your own fruit. What are your strengths? What are your weaknesses? How do you deal with conflict? What area of ministry are you most comfortable? What area of ministry are you uncomfortable with? Knowing the answers to these questions and more will help you to build your confidence and stand firm in your God-given

Self Discovery

identity. People who don't know their identities are oftentimes unstable because they tend to lean to others for affirmation.

2. **Know whose you are.** You can't know who you are until you know who you belong to. You belong to YAHWEH; that's no secret. But do you know Him outside of what you've heard or read about Him? Do you know Him intimately? Do you hear from Him or are you currently relying on others to tell you what He said to you and of you? You've got to have an intimate relationship with God before you can effectively help others to find themselves.

3. **Identify your team.** God has a team of people He will assign to you, but you've got to know who's been sent by God versus who's been sent by the enemy. The key to knowing your true team is knowing the Word of God, and walking in absolute faith. A leader who walks in fear will oftentimes surround himself or

Self Discovery

herself with the wrong people because fear has deafened them to God's voice. Nevertheless, a leader who walks in faith is a leader who's alert, discerning, and prayerful.

4. **Identify your enemies.** Sometimes, we get so religious in our walks that we neglect to try the spirits who join themselves to our lives and ministries. We become so blinded by what we want that we have trouble seeing what's right in front of us. Pray about the people who link themselves up with you, and learn to identify your enemies so that you won't open your heart or home to them.

5. **Know what seeds to sow and what seeds to uproot.** Launching a ministry is hard enough without having to deal with the constant requests to sow seeds. Our seeds include our time, money, and even providing a platform for another leader to stand on. We've got to know which seeds to sow and which ones to uproot to ensure our

Self Discovery

ministries grow up without incident.

Self discovery is one of the first steps to launching or starting a ministry because you're going to be helping others to discover themselves. Don't become distracted by what others have or appear to have, but stay focused on the kingdom works you're assigned to perform. In order to be a successful minister, you've got to think with the mind of Christ. Christ didn't chase platforms, nor was He motivated by selfish gain. Christ simply loved the people so much that He went about the earth without having the comforts of a home to return to day after day. He wanted to win souls for the kingdom of God, and that's how we all should be. We can't become so distracted by the things this world has to offer that we lose focus on our assignments. Know who you are and what God has assigned you to do. God will elevate you in due season, but again, make sure you don't desire the fame and the glory that so many leaders today are chasing. Please know that those things are nothing but lures the enemy is using to catch

Self Discovery

God's people in temptation. After he's caught a leader, Satan likes to reel them up and show them off to the world and the church because he desires to bring down the church one leader at a time and one congregation at a time.

The Faith to Move Mountains

Have you ever stood before a mountain? If you have, you will have noticed the immeasurable height and width of that mountain, and the idea of moving the mountain seems preposterous. After all, in the natural, it is impossible for a human being to place his hands on a mountain and move it. That's because the carnal man is too weak to move such a great force of nature. Why is that? The average height of a man is five foot, nine inches tall, whereas, the average height of a mountain is over 23,000 feet above sea level, or basically, the top of the sea's surface. Nevertheless, a man can move a mountain, but just not with his natural being. A believer can move a mountain with his faith.

Mark 11:23 (KJV): For verily I say unto you, That whosoever shall say unto this mountain, Be thou removed, and be thou cast into the

The Faith to Move Mountains

sea; and shall not doubt in his heart, but shall believe that those things which he saith shall come to pass; he shall have whatsoever he saith.

In the aforementioned scriptural text, you'll notice that Jesus used a mountain to demonstrate the power of faith. That's because mountains are the tallest natural phenomenons in the world, nevertheless, the sea is the only natural force deep enough to swallow a mountain. Of course, oceans are deeper than seas, but in the biblical text, seas and oceans are used interchangeably.

Why did Jesus use a mountain to demonstrate his point? Because He had to reason with the natural understanding of mankind. He knew that mountains dwarfed man, and people often climbed mountains to get to the other side of them. No one had ever considered moving the mountain because the idea of moving a mountain stood outside the realm of possibilities. To further demonstrate His point, Jesus went on to use one of the smallest and

The Faith to Move Mountains

lightest products of nature to talk about the power of faith. Jesus spoke of a mustard seed. **Matthew 17:20 (NIV):** He replied, "Because you have so little faith. Truly I tell you, if you have faith as small as a mustard seed, you can say to this mountain, 'Move from here to there,' and it will move. Nothing will be impossible for you."

Again, what we see is Jesus using a mountain to demonstrate the power of faith, and this time, He used one of the smallest products of nature to get His point across. A mustard seed, on average, is about one to two millimeters in size, nevertheless, the Lord said that if we have faith the size of a mustard seed, we can tell a mountain to move and it has to obey us.

Have you ever thought about walking up to a mountain and telling it to move? More than likely, your answer is "no", and the reason is you still believe that it's impossible to move mountains, even though you have enough faith to do so. The reason we tend to be intimidated

The Faith to Move Mountains

by what we believe to be impossible is because we don't want to look like we've been touched by the wrong angel. At the same time, even though you may not admit this to yourself, you don't believe you have enough faith to move a mountain, but in truth, you do. The problem isn't having enough faith because if you believe that Jesus Christ is Lord, He died for our sins, rose again on the third day, and is now seated on the right hand of God, you are not lacking in the faith department. The problem is doubt. Doubt opposes faith, and when your doubt is greater than your faith, you empower doubt by giving the strength of your faith to believing the opposite of what God said. Doubt is perverted faith; it's faith in the devil's doctrine. Of course, we know that Satan is the author of lies, therefore, his doctrine is the doctrine of deception, nevertheless, his doctrine is as widespread as the gospel. We have to choose which report we will believe, but whenever we are faced with the mountains of life, our carnal thinking often takes over and we start reasoning with ourselves and leaning to our own understanding. Faith is to trust God, but anytime we lean to our own understanding, we lean to our natural mind, and the natural mind does not trust God. It only trusts what it can perceive. The natural mind of a man is linked to his flesh, but the spirit of a believing man is linked to the Spirit of God.

Proverbs 3:5 (KJV): Trust in the LORD with all thine heart; and lean not unto thine own understanding.

Galatians 5:16-17 (NIV): So I say, walk by the Spirit, and you will not gratify the desires of the flesh. For the flesh desires what is contrary to the Spirit, and the Spirit what is contrary to the flesh. They are in conflict with each other, so that you are not to do whatever you want.

When starting or running a ministry, you are going to face many mountains, and some of those mountains will appear to be impossible to defeat. Some of those mountains will appear to be unmovable, and their size will intimidate your natural man. But anytime you meet something that's impossible for the natural man to move, you move that thing with

The Faith to Move Mountains

faith. To move it with faith, you can't have unbelief.
How powerful is unbelief?

Unbelief caused the Jews to delay their arrival to their promised lands, and they remained in the wilderness for forty years. Some of them even died in the wilderness, meaning, they never saw the promised land.

Hebrew 3:16-19 (NIV): Who were they who heard and rebelled? Were they not all those Moses led out of Egypt? And with whom was he angry for forty years? Was it not with those who sinned, whose bodies perished in the wilderness? And to whom did God swear that they would never enter his rest if not to those who disobeyed? So we see that they were not able to enter, because of their unbelief.

Because of the unbelief of many of the Nazarenes, Jesus could not perform many miracles when He'd visited Nazareth.

Mark 6:1-6 (NIV): Jesus left there and went to his hometown, accompanied by his disciples. When the Sabbath came, he began to teach in the synagogue, and many who heard him were amazed.

"Where did this man get these things?" they asked. "What's this wisdom that has been given him? What are these remarkable miracles he is performing? Isn't this the carpenter? Isn't this Mary's son and the brother of James, Joseph, Judas and Simon? Aren't his sisters here with us?" And they took offense at him.

Jesus said to them, "A prophet is not without honor except in his own town, among his relatives and in his own home." He could not do any miracles there, except lay his hands on a few sick people and heal them. He was amazed at their lack of faith.

Unbelief can cost someone their deliverance. Demons that you should be able to easily cast out may rise up as mountains because your faith has been overwhelmed by your doubt. **Matthew 17:14-21 (KJV):** And when they were come to the multitude, there came to him a certain man, kneeling down to him, and saying, Lord, have mercy on my son: for he is lunatick,

The Faith to Move Mountains

and sore vexed: for ofttimes he falleth into the fire, and oft into the water. And I brought him to thy disciples, and they could not cure him. Then Jesus answered and said, O faithless and perverse generation, how long shall I be with you? How long shall I suffer you? Bring him hither to me. And Jesus rebuked the devil; and he departed out of him: and the child was cured from that very hour.

Then came the disciples to Jesus apart, and said, Why could not we cast him out? And Jesus said unto them, because of your unbelief: for verily I say unto you, If ye have faith as a grain of mustard seed, ye shall say unto this mountain, Remove hence to yonder place; and it shall remove; and nothing shall be impossible unto you. Howbeit this kind goeth not out but by prayer and fasting.

You'll notice that I used the King James translation of Matthew 17:14-21, and the reason I did this is because the New International Version's translation quoted Jesus as saying, "Because you have so little faith," but the King James Version quoted Him as

The Faith to Move Mountains

having said the disciples couldn't cast the demon out of the boy because of their unbelief. Nevertheless, unbelief isn't necessarily a lack of faith; it's oftentimes the presence of doubt. Doubt is often a man's response to his lack of understanding, whereas, faith is a man's response to the presence of Godly knowledge and his confidence in that knowledge. The disciples were men of faith; they believed that Jesus was the Son of God. Their problem wasn't that they lacked faith; their problem lied in them doubting themselves. You see, unbelief often targets self because it's powerful enough to get us to question ourselves, but it's not always strong enough to get us to question God. Peter believed that through the power of God, he could walk on water, but it was when he took his eyes off Jesus that he began to sank. Why is that? Peter noticed the raging winds, and he began to think as a natural man. He took his eyes off Christ and realized that what he was doing was naturally impossible. Peter challenged the law of physics and won because he trusted the Lord, but when Peter's carnal understanding took over, he became

The Faith to Move Mountains

subject to the law. If you'll notice, Peter didn't just drop down in the water as physics would demand, instead, he started to sink. This means that Peter's sinking was gradual. That's because he still had enough faith to keep him afloat, but of course, the more he saw himself sinking, the more he sunk.

How does this apply to our daily lives and ministries? Unbelief goes hand in hand with fear because unbelief is what sets the foundation for fear to stand on. The size of your unbelief measures itself against the height of your faith, and of course, your faith is only as strong as the amount of Word you have in you. If you don't read your bible often or know what the Word of God says, your unbelief will be greater than your faith. So, even though you believe that Jesus Christ is Lord and you can do all things through Christ who strengthens you, you won't be able to move any mountains because your unbelief dwarfs your belief. The size or amount of the Word in you must be greater than the size or amount of doubt in you in order for faith to work. That's why you need

The Faith to Move Mountains

to study the Word of God each and every day until you become a vessel carrying the Word. You need the faith to move mountains if you want to launch a ministry, and you need to have already moved a few mountains to run a successful ministry. Nowadays, there are so many folks running around calling themselves Bishops, Apostles, Prophets, and Pastors, but many of them can't even move a paper bag with their faith. They can preach about faith, but they don't have faith, and this is evidenced in their personal lives. Their marriages are falling apart, their ministries are falling apart, and they can barely keep their bills paid, and the reason they're going through all of this is because they claimed offices that they weren't qualified for. The enemy will always come and test you according to what you claim to be, and if you don't have enough Word in you to stay above sea level with the devil, you will begin to sink. If you claim to be anointed by God, you will be tested by the devil because Satan loves to make a mockery of the church.

To get the faith we need to move, not just

The Faith to Move Mountains

physical mountains, but the mountains that present themselves as giants, trials, and tribulations in our lives, we've got to be filled with the Word of God. The problem these days is that so many leaders fill themselves with their own words, and then, try to throw a few scriptures at their situations, and those situations continue to grow out of control. They do this because they're trying to see which method is effective for them. For example, let's say the devil attacks brother Reggie's marriage, and his wife seems to be complaining about everything he does. Brother Reggie gets frustrated and starts verbally assaulting his wife. He threatens her with divorce, packs his bags, leaves his own home, and even threatens to cut off his wife's financial support. After a few days, brother Reggie grows tired of living with his mother, so he decides to return home, but on his way to his house, he begins to pray. Can you see how hypocritical this is? It's clear that brother Reggie has more faith in his own devices than he does in the Word of God, so he tried his own devices first, and when they didn't produce

The Faith to Move Mountains

the fruit he wanted, he decided to try prayer. How many of us do this in our own lives? When we catch ourselves doing this, we ought to stop in our tracks and rebuke ourselves. If you trust in your own devices more than you trust in the Word, you will deal with unbelief, and you will become imprisoned by your natural understanding or mode of reasoning. What brother Reggie should have done was taken authority over his house and cast the devil out, instead of leaving and letting the devil keep the house he's been paying for. How silly is it that we tend to pay for things, and then, we let the devil kick us out of those things? God said that He would give us lands that we did not labor for, cities that we did not build and vineyards that we did not plant, nevertheless, unbelief will make you turn those things over to the devil. That's why you need the faith to move mountains, otherwise, those mountains will, without a question or a doubt, move you.

If you're looking to launch a ministry or if you're already running a ministry, you've got to build your faith until it runs unbelief away from you.

The Faith to Move Mountains

If you don't get the faith you need to run that ministry, that ministry will end up running you in the ground. Please understand that you're going to be dealing with all types of people, and this means you'll be dealing with all sorts of demonic spirits, and you can't volunteer to address a demon with a master's degree. You need faith to come against that demon, and you need the Word to get the faith you'll need to bind that demon! Look at your life right now and ask yourself if you are moving mountains, or if those mountains are currently moving you. If you're being tossed to and fro like a leaf in the wind, you need more of the Word in you. Get in the Word, meditate on the Word, and make the Word a part of your daily vocabulary. You're studying for one of the greatest tests you'll ever take in your life, and that test is the test of your faith. It is your faith that is going to be placed on trial. If you haven't studied the Word, you will fail that test and you'll have no one to blame but yourself. If there's greatness on the inside of you, you need to study the Word because the Word is the only key that can unlock that greatness. Study the Word

The Faith to Move Mountains

and practice moving mountains whenever you can. Pick a problem in your life and solve it with the Word. Do this until your faith dwarfs your unbelief, and that's when you can say you have the faith to move mountains.

A Prophet Without Honor

Jesus went to his hometown, and the bible tells us that He was unable to perform many miracles amongst the people because of their unbelief. They recognized Jesus as one of themselves, and we know that familiarity often blinds the people of God because when we're familiar with someone, we tend to see them for who they were as opposed to who they are. More than that, when we are familiar with people, we have a hard time seeing God in operation in their lives because our natural man wants to relate to them.

We were all unsaved at some point in our lives, and many of us were some pretty messed up characters. We were the devil's puppets, and we enjoyed showing off our sins and everything that we believed our sins had earned us. For those of us who came through

A Prophet Without Honor

families full of unsaved folks, we were comfortable sitting with our families and discussing our bad choices. We ran from the call on our lives until we couldn't run anymore. When we decided to answer the call on our lives, there were many people who thought our priestly professions of faith were nothing short of comedic. Our friends and family members waited around for us to return to the vomit they knew we once enjoyed, and anytime we fell, they celebrated our falls because they could not fathom the idea of us being new creatures in Christ. Some of us were pimps, prostitutes, drug addicts, money lovers, and witches. To anyone who knew us, it was impossible for us to change, nevertheless, we accepted the call on our lives and God changed us.

Nowadays, many of us avoid preaching in our hometowns because of familiarity. The people who knew the men and women we once were find it hard to accept the new creatures that we are today. They think we're putting on a show because, again, in their minds, it is impossible for someone who was so messed up to change

A Prophet Without Honor

into a minister of the gospel.

Mark 6:4 (NIV): Jesus said to them, "A prophet is not without honor except in his own town, among his relatives and in his own home."

The problem isn't always us not being accepted when we're in the midst of people who are or were familiar with us, the problem is many leaders insist on staying in the realm of familiarity because that's where they're most comfortable at. For example, let's use brother Reggie again. Let's say that brother Reggie's father had a church in their little hometown, and brother Reggie's father leaves that church to brother Reggie. But the folks at the church are divided and no one can seem to respect brother Reggie because they saw how bad off he was when he was growing up. They know how much of a headache he'd been to his parents, and many of the older members still see him as that little boy who used to run errands for them. Now that Reggie has grown up, the folks at the church see Reggie as nothing but a young wannabe preacher who doesn't have the wisdom, knowledge or the understanding to fill his father's now empty shoes. Brother Reggie's church is riddled with chaos, disorder, and unruliness; nevertheless, Reggie continues to preach, even though the members of his church aren't benefiting from his teaching. What should he do?

First and foremost, we have to remember that church is not a business to be passed down from one generation to the next because the people may respect our leadership, but have trouble submitting to the leadership of our children. A church should always be placed under the care of whomever the Lord elects to take our places. Nevertheless, many in the church see the building and its members as nothing more than inheritances to pass down to their children, and this mindset is not of God. Wherever familiarity is, there will also be contempt, rebellion, and disorder. This means that, as leaders, we ought to train up our children in the way they should go, meaning, we need to teach them to be effective leaders and never subject themselves to familiarity.

A Prophet Without Honor

Also, as leaders of the gospel, we have to be very careful that we don't get too personal with the members of our churches. I know that some people will see this statement as one birthed in pride, but it is not. If you've been in leadership long enough, you will know the damage familiarity can do to a ministry. People can receive more from you when they are not familiar with you personally than they could if you were hanging out with them. No, we should never place ourselves above the people or think we can't serve them, because Jesus served the people. Nevertheless, we have to always keep in mind that we are watching out for their souls, and as such, we can't entertain personal relationships with people, knowing fully well that those relationships will hinder the people. After all, we are not perfect creatures, but sometimes, the members of our churches see the good in our lives, and they strive to be better because of what they see with us. Let's say that brother Reggie has a church, a wife, and three children. He has a nice home, a pretty good job, and his life looks immaculate from the outside. Brother Reggie does not look like what he's been through, so many people who didn't see him when he was going through thinks his life is nothing short of perfect. Brother Reggie preaches about the struggles he's faced in the past and some of the struggles he's currently facing, nevertheless, many people in the congregation are going through something far worse than what brother Reggie is going through. They don't know that in the past, brother Reggie went through something far worse than what they are going through, so they see brother Reggie's current problems are minuscule. They look at the Pastor's life and think that he's attack-proof, so they listen to what he teaches since he's testified that he's gone through many of the storms they're facing.

One day, brother Reggie gets personal with one of the members named brother Richard. Richard admires what he believes to be Reggie's life, so before the Pastor had gotten personal with him, Richard trusted him with his soul. As time goes on, brother Richard and

A Prophet Without Honor

Pastor Reggie grow closer, and before long, the good Pastor starts sharing the details of his struggles in marriage with newfound friend. As it turns out, Pastor Reggie's life isn't so perfect after all. He's just discovered that his teenage daughter is pregnant, his son has been expelled from school, and to top matters off, his wife is planning to leave him. Now, all of these things does not mean that Reggie isn't qualified for the office of a pastor; it simply means he's sinking and needs to put his eyes back on Jesus.

After hearing about the pastor's struggles, brother Richard decides that he no longer trusts the good pastor to shepherd his soul because he's had to counsel the pastor a few times. Because of this, brother Richard starts trying to control how Pastor Reggie runs his ministry, and when the pastor rebukes him, brother Richard turns in his letter of resignation. Can you see how this situation came about? The pastor should have turned to whoever he's in submission to for guidance, but instead, he let his emotions lead him in the wrong direction. Now, he's lost a member of his church and the respect of that member. At the same time, it is likely that brother Richard is going to share what he knows about the pastor with others because he wants to justify his choice to excommunicate himself from the ministry. The pastor's willingness to open himself up to someone who's not qualified to cover him was a mistake, and this mistake has cost so many leaders their ministries. We can never get to the point where we become prophets without honor in our churches.

When Jesus went to His hometown, the people tried to relate to what they knew about Him. Basically, they questioned whether He was qualified to teach or not. It wasn't because Jesus had done anything wrong or even been a rebellious child. The problem was they were familiar with Jesus, the Son of man, and could not see Him as the Son of God.

Mark 6:1-3 (NIV): Jesus left there and went to his hometown, accompanied by his disciples. When the Sabbath came, he began to teach in the synagogue, and many who heard him were

A Prophet Without Honor

amazed.

"Where did this man get these things?" They asked. "What's this wisdom that has been given him? What are these remarkable miracles he is performing? Isn't this the carpenter? Isn't this Mary's son and the brother of James, Joseph, Judas and Simon? Aren't his sisters here with us?" And they took offense at him.

Now, the first thing you should notice is how they tried to relate to Jesus in the natural. All of their questions pertained to Jesus's natural state. The next thing you should make note of is how they felt about Him. The passage tells us they took offense with Him. Were they offended because He'd directly or indirectly offended any of them? No. They were offended with Him because they were familiar with the Son of man, and they thought He wasn't qualified to teach them. Because of this, the Lord did not perform many miracles in Nazareth. Isn't this how our friends and family behave? Many people who know us become offended when we speak the truth to them.

A Prophet Without Honor

What's the most common phrase people use with leaders? The most common statement you are likely to hear is, "Don't preach at me." In other words, what they're saying is, "I don't want to know you as the preacher. I want to speak to you on my level." This is why we have to take extra precaution when initiating personal relationships with people. We have to make sure that we don't become so familiar in the flesh with the sheep we are assigned to lead that we lose their respect. At the same time, it's wise to seek the Lord as to what city, state, county, and country He wants us to set up churches in. That way, we don't end up running barren ministries that have no fruit to show forth when the Lord returns. What happens when a ministry becomes barren? It becomes a religious, law-abiding establishment where people come to perform and be entertained, but no one's coming to be changed by the renewing of their minds. Such churches are houses of rebellion, and this means they are nothing more than religious establishments filled with religious, rebellious people and the witchcraft they call ministry.

A Prophet Without Honor

To be a prophet with honor, you must sit in the midst of the people God has assigned to you. There are too many leaders out today who are trying to hold on to people God is urging them to let go of. These people are familiar with them, and can no longer receive from them. They've become prophets without honor amongst the congregations they are attempting to lead, and when this happens, the proper thing to do is pray and ask God for direction. What you'll find is that whenever you get too familiar with the people, God will often move you and place you over a different congregation. You see, it's not about having the church and retaining the members; the power is in being able to maintain the level of respect needed to be able to lead the people of God. Additionally, please beware of offense. Anytime you see offense, you're likely going to find familiarity or rebellion in the midst, and that's a situation you need to distance yourself from.

To be effective leaders, we have to remember to separate our emotions from our ministries.

A Prophet Without Honor

We can never lead a church emotionally, nor can we be led by our emotions. It won't be easy to disappoint many of the people who will come to you in hopes of establishing a personal relationship with you, but always remember that if they connect to you personally, they'll have trouble connecting to you spiritually. It is at that moment that you're being given a choice between being their leader or being their friend, and if God did not tell you that the person before you is someone He wants you to befriend, you have to maintain your position as their leader. Please understand that some of your church's members will try to connect with you on a personal level because they've got some personal problems they think you can help them with. After all, in the pulpit, you come off as having all the answers. They don't want to make the necessary changes that you often preach about. Some folks think they can chase the things of this world, and then, pray the ruler of this world out of their homes. They're not looking to change; they're looking for ways to maintain their lifestyles without

A Prophet Without Honor

having to read their bibles or obey the Lord. There are so many leaders today whose churches have been shut down repeatedly because they keep getting personally involved with the people they are assigned to lead. Sure, you counsel people, you pray for them, you encourage them, and you rebuke them when they need to be rebuked, but you should never open up your personal life to the members of your church. If you do, they won't be able to submit to your leadership anymore because you've made yourself familiar with them, and a prophet is not honored by the people who are familiar with him or her.

Below, are four things prophets commonly have to leave behind:

- Prophets oftentimes have to leave the towns and the people who are familiar with them. Abraham had to leave his family and the land he'd grown up in. **Genesis 12:1 (NIV):** The LORD had said to Abram, "Go from your country, your people and your father's household to the land I will show you."

A Prophet Without Honor

- Along with the people they are familiar with, prophets oftentimes have to leave behind their personal belongings in order to follow the instructions of God. You'll find that many prophets tend to move from one state to the other until they mature as prophets and figure out that they can live in one state, and travel to another state to fulfill whatever assignments they have in that state. Of course, that is if the assignment isn't a lengthy one. When a prophet hasn't matured, that prophet will often relocate a lot in an attempt to find themselves and fulfill their assignments. When a prophet of God does mature, that prophet will travel a lot, but they won't always see the need to relocate just because they have an assignment in another city, state, or country.
Matthews 19:29 (KJV): And every one that hath forsaken houses, or brethren, or sisters, or father, or mother, or wife, or children, or lands, for my name's sake, shall receive an hundredfold, and

shall inherit everlasting life.
- Prophets often have to leave their old identities behind so they can walk in their designated places. Now, this doesn't necessarily mean a prophet has to change his or her natural name, but they do have to change what they answer to. When Christ revealed to Simon (Peter) who he was, He wasn't just changing Simon's name, He was handing him his purpose. Your name has meaning, and our natural parents often gave us names that were personable to them, but our Godly names are the names directly tied to our earthly assignments.

John 1:40-42 (NIV): Andrew, Simon Peter's brother, was one of the two who heard what John had said and who had followed Jesus. The first thing Andrew did was to find his brother Simon and tell him, "We have found the Messiah" (that is, the Christ). And he brought him to Jesus.

Jesus looked at him and said, "You are

A Prophet Without Honor

Simon son of John. You will be called Cephas" (which, when translated, is Peter).

- Prophets always have to leave their comfort zones. You'll find that most people who have a true prophetic anointing ran from their assignments because they were comfortable in their lives and routines. They did not want to give up what they knew to walk in the unknown. Many prophets found themselves hiding out in ungodly relationships, clubs, and some even hid themselves in powerless churches, hoping to not be identified.

Nevertheless, a prophet on the run from his or her assignment is a prophet who will face many storms until he or she finally surrenders to the call on his or her life.

Jonah 1:1-5 (NIV): The word of the Lord came to Jonah son of Amittai: "Go to the great city of Nineveh and preach against it, because its wickedness has come up before me." But Jonah ran away from the Lord and headed for Tarshish. He went down to Joppa, where he found a ship bound for that port. After paying the fare, he went aboard and sailed for Tarshish to flee from the Lord. Then the Lord sent a great wind on the sea, and such a violent storm arose that the ship threatened to break up. All the sailors were afraid and each cried out to his own god. And they threw the cargo into the sea to lighten the ship.

Many of you have the call of the prophet on your lives or you operate in the prophetic, but you tend to shy away from that gift because it looks intimidating to you. Trying to run away from the office you're called to is like trying to run away from your own shadow. You are who you are, and the sooner you make peace with that, the sooner you will find peace. Even if you continue trying to fit in with your family and friends, one thing you'll notice is that no matter how sinful you are, you just can never seem to fit in. That's because you were set apart from

A Prophet Without Honor

them, so your attempts to fit in are nothing more than poorly scripted performances. Again, you are who you are and there's no getting around that. You won't fit in with the people you love and you will be rejected by many people, but you should be used to that by now. After all, most prophets started dealing with rejection early in life, and this was to prepare them for their assignments. A prophet's attempt to fit in only makes him or her stand out more. If God called you as a prophet, you are a prophet; just make sure that you are a prophet with honor and not a prophet without honor. Please know that regardless of where you go and what you do, the enemy knows you have an assignment to tear down his kingdom, and if you run from that assignment, the enemy won't feel any less intimidated by you. That's because he knows you can turn around at any given time and accept the call on your life. So, prophets who are outside the will of God still undergo vigorous and unmerciful attacks from the enemy, but prophets inside the will of God are opened to hear from God and avoid many of

A Prophet Without Honor

those attacks. You see, God told many of the prophets of the bible what lands they were to avoid. He did this because He was protecting them. Can you imagine a prophet who has entered rebellion and deafened his ears to the voice of the Lord? That prophet would find himself going through many storms without the power to rebuke those storms or the instructions to get out of those storms. You need God, and there's no way to get around who you are. A prophet is still a prophet, whether that prophet is in the will of God or in rebellion, but a prophet with honor is an effective prophet who brings good news, instructions, and warnings to the people of God. A prophet without honor is rendered almost ineffective because of the dishonor the people have for them. If you can't perform the signs, wonders, and miracles God has designed you to perform, chances are, you're in the wrong place, seated amongst the wrong people. Make sure you are where God has assigned you to be, and make sure that you allow no man or ministry to dishonor you. Always go where you are honored, even if

A Prophet Without Honor

you're not welcomed.

The Truth About 501c3

What is the 501(3)c and how does it affect ministries? According to Wikipedia, a 501c3 is: The most common type of tax-exempt nonprofit organization falls under category 501(c)(3), whereby a nonprofit organization is exempt from federal income tax if its activities have the following purposes: charitable, religious, educational, scientific, literary, testing for public safety, fostering amateur sports ...

Many church leaders are quickly grabbing their pens and unknowingly signing over the rights to their ministries. Here's the truth. Your church should never be recognized as a non-profit organization, an that's because such a status limits the power of your ministry. Basically, it's like placing handcuffs on your ministry, but giving it the power to roam about the earth freely. Many leaders think that in

The Truth About 501c3

order for their churches to be official churches, they must acquire 501c3 status, when this is not true. Churches are not legally recognized, and therefore, are tax exempt. This means that whether you file for official tax exemption through the 501c3 or not, your ministry is automatically tax exempt.

What are the benefits to the 501c3? Truthfully, many people file for this status because:
- Lack of Knowledge- Many leaders think they need a 501c3 to have an official church.
- Deception- Many leaders think that having 501c3 status means they'll automatically get more donations. This is not true.
- False Sense of Accomplishment- Many leaders simply want to feel like their ministries are moving forward and growing, so pursuing 501c3 status makes them feel a false sense of accomplishment.
- Monkey See, Monkey Do- It's no secret that many leaders are following in the

The Truth About 501c3

footsteps of other leaders, and when they see someone they admire or aspire to be like applying for 501c3 status, they follow suit.

Again, churches are already tax exempt, and thereby, not affiliated with the United States government, but when a church obtains 501c3 status, that church is then recognized as property of the state. A lawyer by the name of Barbara Ketay (Biblical Law Center), wrote: *"O.K. Pastors, Evangelists, Missionaries, Deacons, Trustees, Elders... listen up! Let's stop all the hocus-pocus, the illusions, the scams, the fairy-tales and the outright lies regarding what the 501(c)(3) incorporated church is and is not. For a change, let's deal with facts. For those of you who don't understand "facts," in the legal arena, facts are used and are supported by documented evidence which would be admissible in a legitimate court of law. Facts are not hyperbole!"*
She goes on to say the following:
THE down side of the 501(c)(3) corporation:

The Truth About 501c3

- *The creator of a corporation is the State;*
- *The State is the sole authority and sovereign head over the corporation;*
- *The corporation is subject to the laws of the State which limits its powers;*
- *The corporation has no constitutionally protected rights, except 14th Amendment;*
- *The corporation is an artificial person;*
- *The corporation submits to a State Charter declaring it is a creature of the State;*
- *The corporation is created for the benefit of the public;*
- *The corporation is a State franchise;*
- *The corporation is a privilege granted by the State.*

(Reference: Barbara Ketay, "The 501(c)(3) Incorporated Church: The Real Truth," Biblical Law Center).

The 501c3 makes your ministry property of the state and limits its power. At the same time, when you acquire 501c3 status, your ministry is basically regarding the state as its creator, and not God. Can you understand why placing your ministry under the state could be dangerous and unwise? After all, man's government should never rule over God's government. At the same time, many ministers know the downfalls of placing their ministries under a 501c3, but they proceed because, nicely put, they want more money. A lot of large organizations won't donate money to any entities that don't have official documents stating they are tax exempt, and the reason behind this is they want to make sure they can write off their donations on their taxes. So, a lot of leaders rush to get the necessary documents to qualify for those donations, not understanding that many large organizations will not donate to religious organizations because they fear that by doing so, they are (politically speaking) acknowledging and agreeing with the beliefs of that religious organization. Giving a donation to a religious organization is too much of a risk for them, so many companies that help ministries and organizations acquire 501c3 status advise them to be as secular as possible and not acknowledge that they are ministries. This is supposed to help increase their chances of getting donations. In other words, they have to denounce Christ for the money. At the same time, registering your ministry as a 501c3 qualifies you to receive private grant money from the government, money you'll likely never see.

Steve Nestor, a Senior I.R.S. Officer said the following about churches applying for tax exempt status through a 501c3:

"I am not the only IRS employee who's wondered why churches go to the government and seek permission to be exempted from a tax they didn't owe to begin with, and to seek a tax deductible status that they've always had anyway. Many of us have marveled at how church leaders want to be regulated and controlled by an agency of government that most Americans have prayed would just get out of their lives. Churches are in an amazingly unique position, but they don't seem to know or appreciate the implications of what it would mean to be free of government control."

The Truth About 501c3

(Reference: Steve Nestor, IRS Senior Officer, IRS Publication 526, quoted by Peter Kershaw, In Caesar's Grip).

There are many people out today who think it's impossible for their ministries to succeed if they aren't under the ruling thumb of a 501c3, but the truth is, you have more power without linking your ministry up to the government than you have once it's linked. Nevertheless, the ultimate decision is up to the man or woman whom God has entrusted to run those ministries, and of course, a lot of people who know they're relinquishing their power to the government through the 501c3 still apply for 501c3 status for various reasons. Whatever you decide to do with the ministry you're entrusted with is your decision, but at least make sure you know what all the 501c3 entails so you can make an informed decision. God has closed a lot of ministries because the leaders keep linking those ministries to the world's system when He wants them to operate separately.

James 4:4 (NIV): You adulterous people, don't

The Truth About 501c3

you know that friendship with the world means enmity against God? Therefore, anyone who chooses to be a friend of the world becomes an enemy of God.

Life and Challenges of a Chosen Person

Matthew 22:1-14 (ESV): And again Jesus spoke to them in parables, saying, "The kingdom of heaven may be compared to a king who gave a wedding feast for his son, and sent his servants to call those who were invited to the wedding feast, but they would not come. Again he sent other servants, saying, 'Tell those who are invited, "See, I have prepared my dinner, my oxen and my fat calves have been slaughtered, and everything is ready. Come to the wedding feast."' But they paid no attention and went off, one to his farm, another to his business, while the rest seized his servants, treated them shamefully, and killed them. The king was angry, and he sent his troops and destroyed those murderers and burned their city. Then he said to his servants, 'The wedding feast is ready, but those invited were not worthy. Go therefore to the main roads and invite to the wedding feast as many as you find.' And those servants went out into the roads and gathered all whom they found, both bad and good. So the wedding hall was filled with guests. But when the king came in to look at the guests, he saw there a man who had no wedding garment. And he said to him, 'Friend, how did you get in here without a wedding garment?' And he was speechless. Then the king said to the attendants, 'Bind him hand and foot and cast him into the outer darkness. In that place there will be weeping and gnashing of teeth.' **For many are called, but few are chosen.**"

First and foremost, we have to discuss what it means to be chosen as opposed to called. In the aforementioned parable, Jesus tells us a story of a king who was having a wedding feast for his son. The king had a list of people he'd invited to his son's wedding, but they refused to come. Some of them made excuses as to why they couldn't come, while others took it upon themselves to ridicule and kill the king's servants. It is clear that the people did not like nor did they respect the king. After his invitations had been rejected, the king told his servants to go out into the highways and byways and invite anyone they could find. They were to invite people who ordinarily wouldn't get invitations from royalty, people who had come from all walks of life. One of the men invited came to the wedding improperly clothed, and the king punished him because it was clear that he did not respect the king's majesty. He did not honor royalty, but instead, chose to present himself in an improper way, and of course, such an act could have set off a rebellious movement against the king from the people. The king responded by having the man imprisoned.

How does this parable fit into our ministries and lives? Look at how God works today. So many of God's most powerful and effective leaders were people you wouldn't expect to see in the pulpits. They are former drug addicts, former prostitutes, murderers, and people from all walks of life. Before the arrival

Life and Challenges of a Chosen Person

of Christ, the Israelites had the Levitical priesthood. If you remember, the Levites were the sons and descendants of Aaron. This means that one had to be born into that lineage to be a Levite, whether they were qualified or unqualified. God had chosen Aaron's lineage to bear the responsibility of the priesthood, but after Christ, God instituted a new order. Many of the people who were once called turned away from God because they'd become so religious that they could not or would not accept Jesus Christ as Lord. As a matter of fact, many of the Pharisees were Levites, and the Pharisees observed the Old Testament law, even though they were religious hypocrites who judged man, but elevated themselves above the law. So, when the Pharisees and many of the Jews rejected Jesus, the Lord sent forth and gathered a harvest of the Gentiles, people who were once abominable people. All the same, even today, many who were called by God have neglected to answer the call on their lives, so God has chosen replacements to assume their assignments. Their replacements are people

Life and Challenges of a Chosen Person

who were once abominable souls, people who've done things that were once deserving of death.

Out of everyone God could have chosen, He decided to choose you to carry out a set of assignments in the earth, but to accept your assignment, you've had to get past many of the giants that once bound your family from generation to generation. Remember, the Gentiles were not a chosen people; they were pagans, and God chose many of them to preach the gospel of Jesus Christ. Can you imagine the filth in the families those chosen Gentiles had come from? Can you imagine how much opposition, persecution, ridicule, and slander they had to face? These were people coming from families who'd once worshipped pagan gods, and all of a sudden, they were out preaching the gospel. They lost their loved ones because of their choice to spread the Word, and even before the Gentiles were invited to partake of the salvation given to us by Christ Jesus, the disciples of Christ had to walk away from all they knew to follow Him.

Life and Challenges of a Chosen Person

The scriptures tell us of the story of the rich young ruler. This young man approached Jesus asking what he had to do to inherit eternal life, and after the Lord listed the commandments, the young ruler boasted that he'd followed every one of the commandments since he'd been born. Jesus knew what he was lacking, however, so the Lord told him to go away and sell everything he owned. He told him to give his earnings to the poor and follow Him. As the scriptures tell us, the young man was sad and walked away grieved because he was wealthy. He wasn't willing to suffer for Christ's sake. He wasn't willing to give up anything for the gospel. He simply wanted to add to himself without having to take away anything, and because he loved the wealth of the world more than he loved the Lord, he walked away from salvation. The disciples of Christ, on the other hand, had all turned away from their former lives to follow Christ. After the rich young ruler walked away, Christ turned to His disciples and told them that it is difficult for a rich man to enter the kingdom of heaven. He did not say it was impossible for a rich man

Life and Challenges of a Chosen Person

to enter heaven; He said it was difficult. The rich young ruler had no problem following the commandments because he had everything he needed, and we can safely assume that he'd been wealthy all of his life. Christ wasn't telling him to get rid of his wealth for the sake of making him poor; Christ told him to sell everything he had because Christ saw a young man who had not been tried. He was a rich young ruler. He had people fighting on his behalf, and pretty much anything he wanted had been given to him. He didn't know anything about suffering. He'd simply heard about the kingdom of God, and like everyone else, he wanted to go to heaven, but he didn't want to suffer for Christ's sake. In other words, he was offering the Lord a conditional relationship with himself. He wanted to know what works he had to do to get to heaven, but he was not prepared for the Lord's answer. He thought he'd be given an easy set of instructions, and he could rest assured that his near perfect life on earth would be followed by a perfect eternity in heaven.

Life and Challenges of a Chosen Person

After watching the events unfold and listening to Jesus talk about the difficulties of the rich to enter heaven, Peter reminded Jesus of the sacrifice he and the disciples had made for the gospel.

Matthew 19:27-30 (ESV): Then Peter said in reply, "See, we have left everything and followed you. What then will we have?" Jesus said to them, "Truly, I say to you, in the new world, when the Son of Man will sit on his glorious throne, you who have followed me will also sit on twelve thrones, judging the twelve tribes of Israel. And everyone who has left houses or brothers or sisters or father or mother or children or lands, for my name's sake, will receive a hundredfold and will inherit eternal life. But many who are first will be last, and the last first.

Christ was telling Peter about the reward that would be given to the just. In heaven, we will receive rewards based on the lives we've lived and the choices we've made. That's why Christ spoke of the measure of the reward that people who'd left their families and homes for

Life and Challenges of a Chosen Person

His name's sake would receive once they'd arrived in heaven. Those who are chosen aren't just chosen to sit still; they are chosen to go forth in the earth and preach the gospel of the kingdom of God. Christ even acknowledged that we would lose loved ones and material things for the gospel's sake, but we'd be rewarded in heaven. That is to say, we can expect opposition if we plan to get in the positions He's availed to us. We can expect to lose a lot in order to gain more in return. These things are expected, so why is it that so many of us let offense keep us from obeying God?

I don't think I've ever met a chosen person who hasn't been through their fair share of hurt, betrayal, persecution, rejection, and the like. Some of us have been through more trials than others, but none of us have had to endure more than we could bear. Every chosen person I've met has found themselves the victims of some of life's hardest challenges, but they've emerged from those challenges refined, renewed, and eventually, God restored them. In order to become conquerors, we've got to first engage in war, or in our cases, warfare. Warfare is to be expected. We are more than conquerors through Christ Jesus, but this does not mean we won't have to deal with opposition, adversaries, and competitors. You see, it's the opposition that will determine how far we are willing to go in the Lord. Many have turned back to the world after the enemy viciously, and sometimes slightly, opposed their ministries. So many have fallen to church hurt and betrayal, and they've abandoned their God-given assignments because they were not willing to suffer for Christ's sake.

Philippians 1:29-30 (NIV): For it has been granted to you on behalf of Christ not only to believe in him, but also to suffer for him, since you are going through the same struggle you saw I had, and now hear that I still have.

Acts 5:39-42 (ESV): So they took his advice, and when they had called in the apostles, they beat them and charged them not to speak in the name of Jesus, and let them go. Then they left the presence of the council, rejoicing that they were counted worthy to suffer dishonor for the name. And every day, in the temple and from house to house, they did not cease teaching and preaching that the Christ is Jesus.

Romans 8:17 (NIV): Now if we are children, then we are heirs--heirs of God and co-heirs with Christ, if indeed we share in his sufferings in order that we may also share in his glory.

If you are chosen by God, you can expect to be opposed by the devil. You can expect to suffer for Christ's sake, but the problem with the average believer is they see their opposition as a bad thing. The Apostles rejoiced that they'd been counted worthy to suffer for His name's sake, and if you knew how they beat those men, you would not (in your natural mind) be able to understand how they'd left those beatings rejoicing about having gotten beaten. And even though they'd gotten beaten and warned, the Apostles continued to share the gospel they were commanded not to share.

One mindset that hinders so many chosen believers is the victim mentality. Please

Life and Challenges of a Chosen Person

understand that most, if not all, people who've been chosen by God to complete an assignment in the earth have been through some pretty challenging and intense trials. That's because we have to be prepped to do what God has chosen us to do. A person who's never been through opposition will likely quit at the first sight of trouble, but a person who's gone through opposition and survived it will not fear any of the opposing forces that comes their way. Why is this? Because they know they'll get past that opposition. They've gone through it all before, so a challenge, to them, is nothing more than a season of difficulty, but they know they will come out of it eventually. For example, think of some of the people who have previously had the flu. If they catch the flu again, they won't see the flu as the signature on their death certificates. Instead, they'll understand that the flu is going to hinder them from doing some of the things they want to do until that ailment has run its course. They'll understand that flu symptoms often last for a little over a week or less, so they'll rearrange their plans to give themselves time to heal. Now, imagine a person who's never had the flu before, and that person suddenly catches the flu. Now, if you've ever had the flu, you know its symptoms can be pretty dreadful. That person who's never had influenza may think the disease is going to kill them because they've never felt the effects of the disease before. Life's challenges work the same way. A person who's never suffered through a demonic attack, for example, will likely believe they won't survive the attack, whereas, a person who has gone through an attack may often be heard saying, "This too shall pass."

Whenever we've found ourselves going through the challenges, betrayals, persecutions, rejections, and all that comes with being a minister of the gospel, we've found ourselves having to choose the proper ways to respond to those challenges. In many cases, we didn't choose the best response, and in many cases, we responded in ways that made our Father in Heaven proud. Nevertheless, it was at those times that we were given the opportunities to forgive the people who'd rallied up against us or to walk in the spirit of unforgiveness towards them. Those who chose to walk in unforgiveness made that dangerous choice because they'd submitted themselves to the victim mentality. Instead of understanding that they are chosen, and they are being prepped to carry out the assignments God has given them, they became distracted by one of the tools the enemy used to offend them. They didn't understand who they were in Christ, so they tapped into what they knew to address the people who'd offended them.

A person who's chosen by God has to remain free of unforgiveness, strife and offense, but that's not always an easy task. One of the reasons people often find it difficult to get past offense is because the flesh wants to respond to what it sees, when the real war is in the realm of the spirit. Wisdom opens our eyes to see the real opponent, rather than seeing the vessel the opponent is using to oppose us through.

Life and Challenges of a Chosen Person

Some of the most common challenges chosen people go through or have gone through include:

1. Rejection from one or both parents. Please know that people will often reject what they don't understand, therefore, a person who's chosen by God was chosen before they were in their mother's womb. When they're born, they are foreign to their parents, if their parents are not saved. Instead of loving and nurturing their children, those parents reject and condescend their children simply because those children are foreign to them.
2. Rejection at school. Many people who are chosen by God has had to deal with their fair share of rejection, and this includes rejection from their peers. That's because a chosen person is sanctified, or, in other words, set apart by God. As such, they could not fit into the groups, cliques, and clubs they once wanted to be a part of.
3. Rejection in the workplace. It's not

uncommon for a believer to face ridicule and persecution in the workplace, and oftentimes, this opposition comes from their supervisors. At the same time, they face opposition from their co-workers as well because the anointing on their lives is intimidating to others. Rejection in the workplace is nothing more than the manifested evidence that they've been accepted by God, and therefore, rejected by man. A person who believes themselves to be chosen, but does not face opposition is a person who chose themselves.

4. Betrayal by close friends. One of the problems today is even though there is nothing new underneath the sun, many believers are ignorant of Satan's devices. All too often, believers have people in their lives and close to their anointings, and they lovingly refer to many of these people as friends. The problem is they haven't prayed about their friends, so the devil is able to send a hosts of hindering spirits into their

lives. These people stay in their lives year after year, hindering them from doing the things God has called them to do, and then, when elevation is on the horizon, those "friends" begin to reveal their true nature.

5. Church hurt. Again, a lot of people don't pray about the people in their lives, nor do they pray about the churches they join themselves to. Many believers move out of emotion, and because of this, they find themselves in church buildings that God is not a part of, and when they try to distance themselves from those ministries, they are often ridiculed, persecuted, demonized, and religiously blackballed.

The Truth About Denominations

Today's ministerial craze is to pick a denomination and label one's church with it. We are so determined to segregate ourselves from other churches that many of us choose our denomination based on what's trending in those days. At one point, the term "non-denominational" was popular and everyone rushed to label their churches as non-denominational establishments, but nowadays, what's trending is the term "inter-denominational".

God never meant for the church to separate itself from one another; He only wants us to separate ourselves from unbelievers. Nevertheless, many leaders want to fit in somewhere, and it's difficult for them to fathom the idea of simply being believers. But what's

The Truth About Denominations

the truth about denominations? How did they surface, and how does God feel about them? First and foremost, we have to understand how Christianity came to America.

A Roman Emperor by the name of Constantine is credited for bringing Christianity to the western world. During the first part of Constantine's reign, many Christians were facing religious persecution and even being killed for their beliefs. Constantine himself was an unbeliever, but when he was in the midst of a battle for control over the Western Roman Empire, he had a change of heart.
Constantine had gone to Tiber's River Mulvian Bridge to face Emperor Maxentius , but before the battle begin, it is said that Constant looked in the sky and saw a flaming, red cross. On the cross were the words, "In this sign, thou shalt conquer." Constantine did win that battle and he credited his victory to the Lord. As a matter of fact, Constantine's mother, Helena, had been Christian and many believe he may have returned to his Christian roots.
Constantine was 42 years old before he

The Truth About Denominations

regarded himself as a Christian.

In 313, Constantine and a Roman Emperor by the name of Licinius issued the Edict of Milan. The Edict of Milan basically made it legal for Christians to worship the living God. Before that time, Christians were largely attacked, and the Roman people killed, persecuted, and exiled many who followed the Christian faith.

Constantine eventually took over the role of the patron of Christianity. Nevertheless, the Romans were largely against Christianity, and they wanted to continue to worship their pagan gods. In 325, Constantine attempted to unify Christianity by calling together the Council of Nicea. He believed that Christianity was the religion that could unify the Roman Empire which was largely divided at that time. The people did not want to give up their pagan worship, so in an effort to get everyone under one accord, Constantine decided to Christianize many of the pagan beliefs. The pagan goddess Isis was replaced by Mary and many of the practices performed in Mithraism, the popular religion at that time, were brought into the Roman Catholic Church and christianized. Other pagans beliefs were absorbed, changed, and implemented in the Roman Catholic church; for example:

- Mary replaced the pagan goddess, Isis, and the terms ordinarily associated with Isis were given to Mary. Those terms included "Queen of Heaven" and "Mother of God."
- Many of the Romans were Henotheists. Henotheists believe that there isn't just one god, but many gods, nevertheless, they reverence one god as the superior or supreme god. In the Catholic religion, the gods were replaced with the saints.
- Mithras, the god of Mithraism, was believed to be in the flesh and blood of bulls. Romans believed that by partaking of the flesh of a bull, they would receive salvation. Like the Catholic Church, Mithraism had seven sacraments. The bull's flesh was substituted by the Lord's Supper and

The Truth About Denominations

Christian communion.

After the Roman Catholic Church was implemented, it continued to grow until it became the governing authority, and no other religion was recognized. The Roman Catholic Church was the government at that time, and its influence spread throughout Europe, eventually making its way to the United States. Nevertheless, before it made its way overseas, the Western Christians and Eastern Mediterranean Christians opposed each other greatly, largely because of doctrinal and cultural differences. This divide eventually led to a split in the Roman Catholic Church in 1054 in a movement regarded as the East-West Schism or the Great Schism. The Eastern branch became known as the Greek Orthodox Church, and they severed all ties from the Roman Catholic Church. Eventually, each church continued to break down as conflicts continued to rise about doctrines and church operations. Today, there are currently 217 Christian denominations recognized in the United States alone. Each denomination was formed because of a divide in another denomination. Basically, what happens is one man decides he doesn't like the policies or teachings of the church he's a member of, so he starts his own religion and people start to follow him.

In the late nineties, a new breed of Christians began to emerge, and they referred to themselves as non-denominational. A non-denominational Christian does not identify him or herself as the member of a Christian denomination, but are instead, their own governing authorities. In 1990, there were less than 200,000 people who identified themselves as non-denominational, but by 2008, that number had grown to more than eight million people. Non-denominational Christianity itself is not a denomination, even though many people see it as such. Non-denominational followers regard themselves as more accepting of believers from all walks of life. The rising of the non-denominational church is brilliant considering Christ did not regard Himself as a religious man, nor did He follow any denominations. Instead, at that time, there were believers and non-believers, but the believers were all supposed to be on one accord. Of course, there were some divides in Christianity then, and this is evidenced in many of the stories found in the biblical text.

1 Timothy 19:20 (KJV): Holding faith, and a good conscience; which some having put away concerning faith have made shipwreck: Of whom is Hymenaeus and Alexander; whom I have delivered unto Satan, that they may learn not to blaspheme. 2 Timothy 2:17-18 answers this question for us.

2 Timothy 2:17-18 (KJV): And their word will eat as doth a canker: of whom is Hymenaeus and Philetus; who concerning the truth have erred, saying that the resurrection is past already; and overthrow the faith of some.

Most people want to know what Hymenaeus and Alexander did that would cause Apostle Paul to turn them over to Satan. 2 Timothy 2:17-18 speaks of Hymenaeus and Philetus's crimes against the faith, even though Paul mentions Alexander in 1 Timothy 19:20.

The Truth About Denominations

Nevertheless, we can rest assured they were all guilty of the same crime. They were obviously trying to launch their own versions of Christianity by saying that the resurrection had already past, meaning, God had already judged the living and the dead. To make matters worse, the trio had garnered followers, and this is evidenced in the conclusion 2 Timothy 2:18 where Paul states that the men had overthrown the faith of some.
Another story about division is recorded in Acts 5:1-11.

Acts 4:32-37: All the believers were one in heart and mind. No one claimed that any of their possessions was their own, but they shared everything they had. With great power the apostles continued to testify to the resurrection of the Lord Jesus. And God's grace was so powerfully at work in them all that there were no needy persons among them. For from time to time those who owned land or houses sold them, brought the money from the sales and put it at the apostles' feet, and it was distributed to anyone who had need. Joseph, a Levite from Cyprus, whom the apostles called Barnabas (which means "son of encouragement"), sold a field he owned and brought the money and put it at the apostles' feet.

Acts 5:1-11 (NIV): Now a man named Ananias, together with his wife Sapphira, also sold a piece of property. With his wife's full knowledge he kept back part of the money for himself, but brought the rest and put it at the apostles' feet.

Then Peter said, "Ananias, how is it that Satan has so filled your heart that you have lied to the Holy Spirit and have kept for yourself some of the money you received for the land? Didn't it belong to you before it was sold? And after it was sold, wasn't the money at your disposal? What made you think of doing such a thing? You have not lied just to human beings but to God."

When Ananias heard this, he fell down and died. And great fear seized all who heard what had happened. Then some young men came forward, wrapped up his body, and carried him out and buried him.

The Truth About Denominations

About three hours later his wife came in, not knowing what had happened. Peter asked her, "Tell me, is this the price you and Ananias got for the land?"

"Yes," she said, "that is the price."

Peter said to her, "How could you conspire to test the Spirit of the Lord? Listen! The feet of the men who buried your husband are at the door, and they will carry you out also."

At that moment she fell down at his feet and died. Then the young men came in and, finding her dead, carried her out and buried her beside her husband. Great fear seized the whole church and all who heard about these events.

The book of Acts 4:32 tells us that all of the believers were on one accord. They were unified, and of course, we know that God loves unity. Nevertheless, a man named Ananias, along with his wife Sapphira, plotted to withhold their money. They were acting in rebellion, and we know that rebellion is a sin of witchcraft. Had their rebellion been tolerated, this would have caused a divide amongst the people, and Peter knew this. Ananias's act of

The Truth About Denominations

rebellion likely meant he did not agree with the message that was being preached, so even though he'd agreed to be one with the people, he'd made up his mind that his money was his money. What caused Ananias to make such a foolish decision? The scriptural text tells us that Satan had filled his heart.

Satan's most effective weapon against an individual is individuality. He understands that God wants His people to walk as a unit, so Satan entices believers by appealing to their selfish flesh. One believer who is walking against a unit of believers is powerful enough to divide the unit. How so? Whatever reasoning Satan used to get them to walk against the unit will be the same reasoning they will use to divide the unit. There is power in unity and Satan is terrified of a church that walks in unity. So, what does he do to keep the churches divided? He introduces believers to the same spirit that Hymenaeus, Alexander, and Philetus were seduced by, and we know that spirit to be the infamous lying spirit. A lying spirit is nothing but a spirit who tells lies.

The Truth About Denominations

A deceiving spirit, otherwise known as the lying spirit, was mentioned in 1 Kings 22:22-23.
1 Kings 21:22-23 (NIV): Finally, a spirit came forward, stood before the Lord and said, 'I will entice him.'

" 'By what means?' the Lord asked.

" 'I will go out and be a deceiving spirit in the mouths of all his prophets,' he said.

" 'You will succeed in enticing him,' said the Lord. 'Go and do it.'

"So now the Lord has put a deceiving spirit in the mouths of all these prophets of yours. The Lord has decreed disaster for you."

Now, if you're not familiar with the story, the issue was that King Ahab (a Jew) had married Jezebel (a Phoenician), and Jezebel had turned Ahab away from serving YAHWEH. Ahab began to serve the gods (devils) that his wife worshipped: Baal and Asherah. Ahab was the king of Israel, and he is remembered as having been one of the most wicked kings to ever reign. Ahab allowed his wife to kill the prophets of God, and he caused Israel (the people of God) to worship Baal. God warned

The Truth About Denominations

Ahab many times about his transgressions, but he would not repent, so God decided to dethrone Ahab by allowing him to be killed. During that time, Ramoth Gilead was being ruled by a king by the name of Aram, and Ahab wanted to bring Ramoth Gilead back under his control, so he plotted to go to war against the land. Just like many of the kings of that day, Ahab summoned his prophets to tell him if he'd be successful if he went up against Ramoth Gilead, and God allowed a lying spirit to enter the mouths of his prophets. The lying spirit told Ahab that he would be successful, and of course, this was a lie. You see, God, himself, cannot tell a lie, but there are some lying spirits on the loose, meaning, they are spirits that go against the spirit of Truth.

When Satan wants to divide a church, he simply sends forth lying spirits, and these spirits are convincing, conniving, and calculating. When they speak, their words sound prophetic in nature, and the natural mind cannot discern between a lying spirit and the spirit of Truth. That's why we have to know the

The Truth About Denominations

Word of God because when we know the Word, we'll have within us the spirit of Truth. Of course, we know that that Catholicism itself was nothing more than Satan's attempt to mix truth with lies because the Roman Catholic Church merged pagan practices with Christian doctrine, and what was born was the mother of religiousness. And from Catholicism, many religious institutions were born, but God started calling His children back to Himself, and this calling led to one of the greatest callbacks in recent history: the establishment of non-denominational institutions.

Nowadays, we have a new movement called interdenominational, and the difference between non-denominational and interdenominational is non-denominational believers refuses to affiliate themselves with individual denominations, whereas, interdenominational believers accept people from many, if not all, denominations. Nevertheless, we know God is not a denominational God, but He is a God of truth, and that's what we're called to follow. So,

The Truth About Denominations

when you're establishing a church, make sure you don't get caught up in the religious fads. Just ask the Lord to lead you in all things, and ask the Lord to keep you in every way. You always want to make sure you are leading God's people in Him, rather than misleading them with your understanding. There is a lot of Godly knowledge that the church has not tapped into because of religiousness, and we know that religiousness is nothing more than man-made traditions inspired by religion. Make sure you draw your inspiration from the Holy Spirit and lead God's people in the way of truth.

Five Fold Ministry Offices

The five fold ministry officers are: Apostles, Prophets, Evangelists, Pastors, and Teachers. Each one of the offices has its own duties, but overall, the purpose of the five fold ministry is to bring together the body of Christ in unity. Their purpose is to help us to understand that we are members of the body of Christ, and as such, we all have a function. When everyone is functioning in their God given assignments, the body is edified, meaning, the body is established and improved.

Ephesians 4:11-16 (KJV): And he gave some, apostles; and some, prophets; and some, evangelists; and some, pastors and teachers; for the perfecting of the saints, for the work of the ministry, for the edifying of the body of Christ: Till we all come in the unity of the faith, and of the knowledge of the Son of God, unto a perfect man, unto the measure of the stature of the fulness of Christ: That we henceforth be no more children, tossed to and fro, and carried about with every wind of doctrine, by the sleight of men, and cunning craftiness, whereby they lie in wait to deceive; but speaking the truth in love, may grow up into him in all things, which is the head, even Christ: From whom the whole body fitly joined together and compacted by that which every joint supplieth, according to the effectual working in the measure of every part, maketh increase of the body unto the edifying of itself in love.

There has been much confusion in the church as to what duties each five fold officer carries, and because of religiousness, many are creating their own titles and offices to carry out their selfish agendas. Nowadays, we hear terms like "master prophet" and "chief apostle" when the Lord only gave us five officers. When a person refers to self as "master" or "chief", that person is attempting to differentiate himself or herself from the others. They are basically saying that they are superior to the rest, when, in truth, Paul was the Apostle whom God used the most, nevertheless, he did not refer to himself, for example, as the chief apostle. He simply did what God commanded him to do.

One thing we must remember is anytime we're called into one of the five fold offices, we are going to see differences between ourselves and others. After all, we are teachers of grace, and as a teacher, you may find yourself in a room with thousands of people who don't know what you know, and that's why you're the teacher. Nevertheless, this means that you have a new fight on your hands, a fight that many of the people in the audience will not understand. You have to fight to remain humble, otherwise, you may get puffed up and start glorifying yourself instead of glorifying the Lord. Anytime you are set apart, you've got to remember that humility is a requirement to fulfill whatever office you're called to, and if you lose that humility, pride will come in right before your fall. Prideful people intentionally or unintentionally erect themselves as idols, causing the sheep under them to worship them and not the Lord. One of the ways you'll know when pride is in your heart is if you ever get to a point where everything you say, think, and do is about promoting yourself and your ministry, but not so much the gospel of Jesus Christ.

What are the purposes of the five fold officers? To understand the duty of each officer, you must understand what the words mean themselves.

- **Apostle:** One who is sent by God; kingdom ambassador.
- **Prophet:** Messenger of God.
- **Evangelist:** Messenger of good tidings.
- **Pastor:** Shepherd.
- **Teacher:** Instructor.

Let's further discuss each office as it pertains to the roles and responsibilities of the officers.

Apostles are disciples of Christ who've been sent to unify the body of Christ and bring the church into order. As leaders of the five fold,

Five Fold Ministry Offices

Apostles were first and will always continue to be disciples of the Lord. True Apostles are intolerant of disorder, false doctrine, and rebellion as they are sent to bring order to the church.

Apostles govern certain churches, often monitoring and rebuking the leaders and members of those churches. Every region is often governed by principalities, and these wicked forces usually influence the behaviors of the people in those regions. An Apostle's assignment is to keep the devil out the church, and an Apostle will often notice a certain trend or behavior that's common within a region. Paul rebuked the Corinthian church for their quarreling. (See 1 Corinthians 1:11). He also rebuked the church of Corinth for their sexual immorality. (See 1 Corinthians 5:1).

As a matter of fact, Paul is the Apostle who is commonly used as a paradigm for the roles of Apostleship. Apostles were often sent to cover the regions and the churches in those regions.

Five Fold Ministry Offices

Prophets are the mouthpieces of God. Unlike Apostles, Prophets don't cover regions, but are instead, sent to warn the people of God or bring good tidings to them. A Prophet hears from God and delivers God's Word to His people. Apostles will often stay in a place, only traveling to the churches that he or she covers, but Prophets are often universal and will have to go wherever they are sent.

Most Prophets unexpectedly have their lives interrupted by prophetic orders, and therefore, Prophets don't always do well with jobs that keep them stationery. They need to be free to move whenever God tells them to move. True Prophets speak under the direction of the Holy Spirit, and they don't always tell you what you want to hear. That's why it's easy nowadays to differentiate a true Prophet from a self-sent Prophet because the self erected ones rarely speak of repentance, nor do they rebuke the people of God. Instead, they basically tell them that God is about to bless them in their mess. True Prophets warn the people of God and encourage them to repent so they can receive the blessings of God.

2 Kings 17:13 (NIV): The LORD warned Israel and Judah through all his prophets and seers: "Turn from your evil ways. Observe my commands and decrees, in accordance with the entire Law that I commanded your ancestors to obey and that I delivered to you through my servants the prophets."

A few examples of Prophets delivering messages from God includes:
- Moses was God's Prophet, and he was sent by God to tell Pharaoh to let God's people go.
- Joseph was God's Prophet and he was taken by force to Egypt where he, through the power of God, interpreted the dreams of Pharaoh, and eventually became Pharaoh's second in charge.
- Anna, the daughter of Penuel, was a Prophetess who prophesied about the coming of Jesus Christ. (See Luke 2:36-38).
- Daniel was a Prophet of the Lord who interpreted the dreams of the king after

Five Fold Ministry Offices

he, along with other children of Judah, had been taken into Babylonian captivity. Although commanded not to pray by the Babylonian king, Darius, Daniel disregarded the king's orders and continued to pray to God. For his crime, he was thrown in the lions' den, and of course, if you know the story, God shut the mouths of the lions so they did not eat Daniel.

- Elijah was a Prophet of God who God used to confront Ahab and Jezebel about their crimes against God. King Ahab and Queen Jezebel were rulers over Israel and caused Israel to stumble by leading them into Baal worship. God sent Elijah forth to confront Ahab and to demonstrate His irrevocable power to His people. Elijah is also the Prophet who didn't die, but was instead, taken up by God in a whirlwind.
- John the Baptist was a Prophet sent to prepare the hearts and minds of the people for the arrival of the Christ.

Other renowned Prophets include Miriam,

Five Fold Ministry Offices

Jonah, Samuel, David, Micaiah, Joshua, Noah, Abraham, Elisha, Enoch, Hosea, Isaiah, Samuel, and the list goes on.

Prophets were always sent to prepare the way for a move of God. Warning comes before destruction, so no land could be destroyed before a Prophet warned the people of that land.

Evangelists are ministers of the gospel who reach out to the unsaved, whereas Prophets are sent to warn, rebuke, or encourage the saved. Like Prophets, Evangelists are often ministers who operate outside the four walls of the traditional church. Nevertheless, Evangelists aren't always sent into certain lands because the unsaved are everywhere. Evangelists are ministers of grace who simply go out into the streets to tell the unsaved the good news, and that good news is Jesus Christ died for their sins, and they can now obtain salvation through Him. The disciples of Jesus were all Evangelists before they became Apostles. They went out into the highways and byways with Christ to win souls for the kingdom of God.

Mark, Matthew, Luke, and John are regarded as Evangelists because they published the good news of Jesus Christ.

A great example of an Evangelist is Philip. Bible Study Tools said the following of Evangelists: *a "publisher of glad tidings;" a missionary preacher of the gospel (Ephesians 4:11). This title is applied to Philip (Acts 21:8), who appears to have gone from city to city preaching the word (Acts 8:4 Acts 8:40). Judging from the case of Philip, evangelists had neither the authority of an apostle, nor the gift of prophecy, nor the responsibility of pastoral supervision over a portion of the flock. They were itinerant preachers, having it as their special function to carry the gospel to places where it was previously unknown. The writers of the four Gospels are known as the Evangelists.*
(Reference: www.biblestudytools.com/dictionary/evangelist)

Five Fold Ministry Offices

Pastors are also known as shepherds of God's people. Each Pastor tends to a flock, or, in other words, a select group of people. To better understand a Pastor, you need to understand the role of a shepherd. A shepherd leads, protects, feeds, corrects and nurtures his flock. Peter gave a detailed description of what a shepherd does in 1 Peter 5:1-4.

- **1 Peter 5:1-4 (NIV):** To the elders among you, I appeal as a fellow elder and a witness of Christ's sufferings who also will share in the glory to be revealed: Be shepherds of God's flock that is under your care, watching over them—not because you must, but because you are willing, as God wants you to be; not pursuing dishonest gain, but eager to serve; not lording it over those entrusted to you, but being examples to the flock. And when the Chief Shepherd appears, you will receive the crown of glory that will never fade away.

As Peter mentioned, one of the roles of a Pastor is to set an example for the people he or she is shepherding. This means Pastors don't just lead with their words, they lead with their actions. Unlike Prophets and Evangelists, Pastors aren't normally traveling from one region to another, but are instead, entrusted to guide a select group of believers.

Teachers are people who are well versed in the Word of God, and are assigned to teach or exhort the body of Christ. Paul considered himself both an Apostle and a Teacher as evidenced in 1 Timothy 2:7.

- **1 Timothy 2:7:** Whereunto I am ordained a preacher, and an apostle, (I speak the truth in Christ, and lie not;) a teacher of the Gentiles in faith and verity.

Paul was qualified to teach because he had walked with the Word, Himself. He knew the Word, and therefore, could explain the scriptures in full detail. Teachers and Pastors are similar, but the difference is Teachers don't always have a flock to shepherd, and therefore, are ministers without walls.

Five Fold Ministry Offices

Teachers teach through any available avenue, often getting revelation knowledge from God, and preparing that knowledge for the people of God in ways they can receive it.

Teachers also monitor their students' progress, often checking in to ensure they not only continue learning the Word, but have a full understanding of what they are learning. Because they are breaking down the Word in ways that people can understand it, God strictly judges Teachers because what they share with His people can nurture or poison them.

James 3:1 (NIV): Not many of you should become teachers, my fellow believers, because you know that we who teach will be judged more strictly.

Most Pastors are Teachers as well, but not all Teachers are Pastors. Understanding the roles and responsibilities of the offices we hold helps us to be more effective leaders to the flock we are assigned to. Today, a lot of people don't understand the roles or purpose of

Five Fold Ministry Offices

the five fold ministry, therefore, many people rise up and call themselves Apostles and Prophets, but there aren't too many people who call themselves Teachers. That word has almost become extinct in the vocabulary of modern day ministers. When we accept our true roles, we are not only more effective leaders, but we also have more success in our personal lives. Many leaders today go through much scandal because they aren't operating in their rightful offices, so when the enemy comes to test them, they fail those tests miserably. We've got to understand that we will be tested according to the offices we hold, and, at the same time, we will be judged by the words that proceeded out of our mouths. If we tell people that we are Prophets, for example, and God did not call us to the office of the Prophet, we will have to answer for our lies. Nowadays, the enemy has launched one of his most effective campaigns against the church by sending out many false apostles and prophets to mimic the true ones. False leaders mislead the people of God and cause them to stumble. They are the ones on the news leading so many people to follow after themselves, commit mass suicides, commit mass murders, and sin against the living God. Many of the false leaders are the ones involved in scandals, and the devil uses these scandals to discredit the church itself.

If you are called to the five fold ministry, you need to understand your role and responsibility, have a teachable spirit, and be able to humbly receive correction. Even Apostles are subject to correction. Remember, Paul rebuked Peter, also known as Cephas, because Peter was doing what a lot of leaders do today: In the presence of other leaders, he separated himself from the Gentiles and refused to eat with them, but when the leaders were away, he had no problem eating with them. Peter was worried about what the other leaders would think of him, so, in a sense, he was on his way to becoming a people pleaser. **Galatians 2:11-14 (NIV):** When Cephas came to Antioch, I opposed him to his face, because he stood condemned. For before certain men came from James, he used to eat with the Gentiles. But when they arrived, he began to

Five Fold Ministry Offices

draw back and separate himself from the Gentiles because he was afraid of those who belonged to the circumcision group. The other Jews joined him in his hypocrisy, so that by their hypocrisy even Barnabas was led astray. When I saw that they were not acting in line with the truth of the gospel, I said to Cephas in front of them all, "You are a Jew, yet you live like a Gentile and not like a Jew. How is it, then, that you force Gentiles to follow Jewish customs?

No leader is above correction, and any leader who refuses correction is a pride-filled leader whose fall is inevitable.
Proverbs 16:18 (NIV): Pride goes before destruction, a haughty spirit before a fall.

Remember, the purpose of the five fold is:
- to equip God's people for works of service
- to build up (edify) the body of Christ
- to perfect the saints

Our roles and responsibilities are important because there are souls out there who we are

Five Fold Ministry Offices

accountable for. We must fully understand each individual role so that we can better serve our offices. The five fold ministry isn't a thing of the past, as some theologians would have you believe, but it is the established order of God's church today.

The Office of the Bishop

The office of the Bishop is one of the most misunderstood offices to date. Many don't know the difference between a Bishop and an Apostle, so they use the terms interchangeably, nevertheless, the two are not one in the same. Some have even argued that Pastors and Bishops are one in the same, but this is not entirely true.

A Bishop is an elder who's been entrusted to oversee churches, and of course, most elders are Pastors, but a Bishop is a Pastor who's been appointed to the office of a Bishop. This means that not all Pastors are Bishops, but all Bishops should have first been Pastors. As a matter of fact, the words Bishop and Overseer are synonymous. Even though this role is often misunderstood, the Bible gives a clear definition to the office of the Bishop.

The Office of the Bishop

Titus 1:6-9 (NIV): An elder must be blameless, faithful to his wife, a man whose children believe and are not open to the charge of being wild and disobedient. Since an overseer manages God's household, he must be blameless—not overbearing, not quick-tempered, not given to drunkenness, not violent, not pursuing dishonest gain. Rather, he must be hospitable, one who loves what is good, who is self-controlled, upright, holy and disciplined. He must hold firmly to the trustworthy message as it has been taught, so that he can encourage others by sound doctrine and refute those who oppose it.

Roles and Responsibilities of the Bishop
1. **The Bishop must be an elder-** Elders and Pastors are one in the same, but in many traditional churches, Elders are regarded as the older men who basically serve as co-pastors to the Pastor. But in the biblical text, the words Elder and Pastor are used interchangeably, and therefore, have the same responsibilities.

The Office of the Bishop

2. **A Bishop must be blameless-** Because Bishops are overseers and are entrusted to oversee the operations of certain churches, they are required to, in layman's terms, practice what they preach. People cannot respectfully follow hypocritical leaders, so Bishops are required to lead by example.
3. **A Bishop must have one wife, and he must be faithful to his wife-** Again, a Bishop must practice what he preaches, and because he oversees the operations of one or more churches, his responsibilities are to rebuke anyone who is out of order. Christ told us to not attempt to remove the plank from someone else's eyes if we, ourselves, have a plank in our own eyes. Many people have disputed whether a woman can be a Bishop, and even though the biblical texts does not speak on this subject, it clearly said Bishops must be the husbands of one wife.
4. **A Bishop must be able to properly manage his home and have orderly**

The Office of the Bishop

children- Every minister's first ministry is at home, but Overseers are required to have properly managed their own homes before attempting to manage God's people. Again, this is because he must lead by example.

5. **A Bishop must not be overbearing-** What does it mean to be overbearing? Google defines "overbearing" as: *unpleasantly or arrogantly domineering. In other words, a Bishop must be humble and cannot be unpleasant or controlling.*

6. **A Bishop cannot be quick-tempered-** The bible tells us that the Lord is slow to anger, which means, we should all be slow to anger, especially those who are in leadership. All the same, Bishops deal with a lot of people, and as such, they deal with various personalities and strongmen. A Bishop must be gentle and loving so that he can effectively lead the people of God without his emotions getting in the way.

7. **A Bishop cannot be a man given to**

wine, or in other words, a drunk- It goes without saying that an Overseer cannot be someone who is a slave to the bottle. After all, drunkenness, according to the bible, is sin.

8. **A Bishop cannot be violent-** Violence and short tempers go hand in hand. Bishops are called to be pleasant and self-controlled, therefore, a violent Bishop is an oxymoron.

9. **A Bishop cannot pursue dishonest gain-** Since Bishops oversee the operations of churches, they will oversee the financial operations of the churches. A Bishop who loves money is a Bishop who will steal from his church, and such behaviors could divide a church and scatter the sheep.

10. **A Bishop must be hospitable and love what is good-** The word "hospitable" means to be kind and welcoming. Additionally, a Bishop cannot love evil, nor should he partake in the fruits of unrighteousness. Instead, he should abhor that which is

evil and love that which is good. In other words, he cannot serve two masters.

11. **A Bishop must be self-controlled, upright, holy and disciplined-** Again, Bishops are Overseers, and as such, lead by example. God said in Leviticus 17:44 (KJV), "For I am the LORD your God: ye shall therefore sanctify yourselves, and ye shall be holy; for I am holy." Holiness is a standard for the office of the Bishop, therefore, a person in rebellion does not qualify for the office. Of course, when we are holy, we will be self-controlled, upright, and disciplined because we are following in the footsteps of the Lord.

12. **A Bishop must remain faithful to what he has been taught so that he can teach the people of God-** Bishops are subject to Apostles, and therefore, cannot go against the teachings of the church they are heading. If a Bishop disagrees with the doctrine being preached, he can bring it to the

The Office of the Bishop

> Apostle's attention, but he cannot teach a different doctrine, otherwise, he is leading the sheep away from the one who is assigned to cover them.

Even though most Bishops started off as Pastors, they aren't necessarily pastoring churches, but are instead, overseeing the operations of certain churches. As mentioned earlier, some people get the roles of the Bishop and the Apostle confused, but the difference is Apostles are sent by God to oversee churches in certain regions, whereas, Bishops are appointed by Apostles to oversee certain churches in their regions. There are many Pastors who, by the biblical standards, do not qualify for the office of the Bishop. For example, a Pastor who's been appointed by God to pastor cannot lose the anointing on his life to pastor a congregation, but he can be rebuked, be re-assigned, or be sat down for a season because of things going on in his personal life. Nevertheless, no one can take the pastoral anointing away from him, so if he repents and gets his life back in order, he can

The Office of the Bishop

resume his pastoral duties at his appointed Apostle's discretion. Nevertheless, he can disqualify himself from becoming a Bishop if he does not meet the biblically established standards for the bishopric. Of course, you'll notice that I keep referring to a Bishop as "he", but that's because Bishops are referred to in the masculine sense in the bible. In today's churches, there are many women who've been ordained to the bishopric, and of course, each organization has its own interpretations of the scriptures, therefore, we can only uphold the standards for the organizations we're assigned to.

Starting a Ministry

In this day and time, there are many people who have been called or chosen, and even though starting a ministry looks relatively easy, it is a challenge. Because of the obstacles often presented when attempting to launch a ministry, many ministers delay start-up. Anytime God chooses a person to carry out a specific task, that person should expect warfare. The problem is many people retreat from the devil when they should be advancing against his kingdom.

But let's say that you are looking to launch your ministry. You're willing to persevere every storm that rages itself up against your fragile life, and you're willing to endure the persecution, the rumors, the rejections and the betrayals that often follow ministers. You love the Lord enough to endure all the ridicule for

Starting a Ministry

His name's sake. First off, congratulations for being willing to stand for our Lord and Savior, Jesus Christ, and secondly, for your willingness to suffer for Him. Truthfully, there are many false teachers arising, and what usually separates them from true teachers is their unwillingness to go through anything that would dare to threaten life as they know it. Anytime a false teacher is tried with fire, that teacher doesn't come out of the fire refined, he or she comes out redefined, meaning, they are not proven to be whatever they're claiming to be. Many people are willing to go through a few moderate storms here and there, but when the devil comes up against them in full force, they retreat.

In this book, we discussed the challenges of the called and the chosen, and we also talked about how to overcome those challenges, nevertheless, you can't overcome a mountain you weren't anointed to claim. This means you'd better be in the office God assigned you to, otherwise, you will be faced with opposition that you're not equipped for. Ministry is not for

Starting a Ministry

the faint at heart, nor is it the religious pageant so many people have made it out to be. Ministry is a call to service, and we are the soldiers in the army of the Lord. We cannot take our assignments lightly, nor can we make a mockery of the offices God has assigned us to. We've got to always make sure to protect the reputation of the ministerial offices as well as our own names because the devil is looking for incidents to discredit us.

Before you launch your ministry, be sure to prepare yourself mentally, physically, and spiritually for your new journey. Additionally, be sure to prepare your loved ones and help them to understand their roles and responsibilities. Below are ten tips to ministry start-up:

1. **Know who you are in Christ.** What office were you called to? Did the Lord tell you that you were called into that office or did man tell you? If you heard it from a person, did you take it to the Lord first? It is very important that we know who we are in Christ, otherwise,

we'll try to serve in offices that we are not appointed to serve in. Be sure to pray and get clarification from the Lord as to what you are supposed to be doing, and when you're supposed to start doing it.

2. **Know who you're supposed to be submitted to.** One of the main reasons a lot of believers suffer through what is commonly referred to as "church hurt" is because they join themselves to ministries and ministers out of emotion rather than praying and being led by the Holy Spirit of God. A lot of people don't want to follow the ministries God has assigned them to because those ministries challenge them. But going to a church that does not challenge how they think is like being twelve years old and choosing to go back to the first grade. They get to go and hear what they already know, and there is no accountability at the churches they feel most comfortable at. At the same time, a lot of people don't know who they are

supposed to be submitted to, and whenever you submit to the wrong person, that person can and will hinder your walk with Christ. How so? Some people have David-size anointings, and they end up serving under people with Saul-sized demons. Whenever the Lord opens their eyes and they decide to come from under those people, they suffer through some major warfare. It is not uncommon to see a minister who's been criticized and demonized by the leaders he or she was once in submission to.

3. **Understand the role of the office you're assigned to.** It's one thing to know who you are, but understanding the role of the office you're assigned to is just as important. Why is that? Because a lot of people, including people in leadership, have their own misguided interpretations as to the roles of certain ministerial offices. If you don't understand the role of the office you're assigned to, you may take on their

understanding, and they'll have you so far outside the will of God that you will be an ineffective leader. Sure, they will be held accountable by God for misleading you, but you will be held accountable for allowing them to mislead you. Think of it this way. If your older brother told you to jump in a ditch full of mud, your parents wouldn't just punish him, they'd punish you too because you shouldn't have listened to him. God works the same way. As leaders, we should all have an intimate relationship with God, and our relationship with Him should be so powerful that we can talk to and hear back from Him ourselves. When you know your Father's voice, you won't follow the voice of a stranger.

4. **Write the vision and make it plain.** What is the strength of your ministry? Will you have a church building or will you be a church without walls? What's your vision for your ministry? How many people do you believe God will

seat under you, and how are you preparing for their arrival? Believe it or not, writing the vision makes it easier to implement. The best thing to do is get a journal and start to write whatever vision God gives you for the ministry. Don't be distracted by other ministries, what they have or what they do not have. Just focus on being properly aligned with God's plan for your ministry.

5. **Get the legal stuff taken care of.** You've got to understand the laws of your state as well as federal laws governing ministries. Find out what paperwork you have to file, and be sure to file them promptly. If you don't know how to properly fill out the paperwork, don't hesitate to hire an attorney to help you with the task. Remember, Satan is looking for whomever he can devour, and if you neglect to get whatever licenses and permissions you need to get, you've just handed your ministry to Satan for consumption.

6. **Build your team.** Your team will help

Starting a Ministry

you to take your ministry from one level to the next, and that's why it's very important to pray about the people in your circle. At the same time, use your God-given discernment, and don't just give people positions just because they're talented or willing to accept those positions. You need a team of faithful, God-fearing souls around you so that you won't end up with a Judas in your camp. Just minister however God has told you to minister and wherever He has told you to minister, and He will bring your team together. Again, let me reiterate this because it's very important: Don't just invite folks in just because you see how beneficial they can be to your ministry because sometimes the folks who have the most to offer have the least to lose, and people like that can be dangerous. Remember, Satan won't always send folks who look like they need deliverance. Some of the most dangerous saints are the ones who look like they're already delivered.

Starting a Ministry

7. **Brand your ministry.** Branding your ministry is important because we live in a time where the large majority of people in western and some eastern countries are turning to the media for help making their decisions. This includes people who are looking for church homes. When you brand your ministry, what you're doing is basically inviting the people to come to your church. Your website serves as a visual front for those who are considering visiting your church. Your flyers inform people of your church's locations and events. Your videos give people a preview of what they can expect if they were to come to your church. Nowadays, people rely on branding, and for this reason, the fields of marketing and graphic design are continually changing and expanding. This is a great time to take advantage of the many branding tools available for us, and this includes getting your website, mobile app, press release, flyers,

business cards, and videos professionally designed. Make sure you look around for professional designers who can help you put a face on your brand.

8. **Get the necessary funding.** Your ministry's start-up and running requires funding, and unfortunately, getting people to fund ministries can be pretty arduous. Today's media shines an unfavorable light on ministers and ministries who ask for help funding their ministries, and for this reason, we've got to be careful how we ask for help getting the funds we need to build our visions. Many churches file for 501c3 status to help motivate people to give to their ministries, but truthfully, we don't need 501c3 status. A 501c3 basically declares the ministry a not for profit organization, therefore, anyone who gives a donation to that organization could write off those donations on their taxes. One thing many don't know is churches are already tax exempt

according to the IRS Code § 508(c)(1)(A) which reads: Special rules with respect to section 501(c)(3) organizations.

> (a) New organizations must notify secretary that they are applying for recognition of section 501(c)(3) status.
>
> (c) Exceptions> (1) Mandatory exceptions> Subsections (a) and (b) shall not apply to— (A) churches, their integrated auxiliaries, and conventions or associations of churches.

You don't need a 501-3c because it actually puts you under the ruling thumb of the United States government, whereas, churches are currently considered independent agencies. You can get the funding you need by simply obeying God and going to wherever He sends you, preaching whatever message He gives you, and being willing to sow whatever seeds He tells you to sow. Other leaders will have you

Starting a Ministry

thinking you need to make a bunch of unnecessary sacrifices to fund your ministry, but with God, obedience is better than sacrifice. There are many things you can do to raise money including hosting events, launching fundraisers, having garage sales, and the list goes on. Also, be sure to look for ministry partners who'll help fund the ministry.

9. **Look for kinks in your ministry, and promptly straighten them out.** We all know that Satan is going to send folks our way to test us and to shine a negative light on our ministries. If you are truly anointed by God, you will be tested, and there's no way to get around this. But wisdom isn't found in getting around the mountain; wisdom is found in moving the mountain out of your way. One of the first things you have to do is pay attention to the people on your team, and always be on the lookout for the hell-raisers. The hell-raisers are the ones who are emotionally handicapped,

Starting a Ministry

people who are easily offended and always trying to tell the leadership how to do their jobs. When you come across one of these souls, the proper way to deal with them is to lovingly, but firmly let them know that their antics will not be tolerated. Give them a set of instructions and rebuke them anytime they start trying to control people with their emotions. It goes without saying, many people who are like that are in much need of deliverance and should not be on the ministry team. For this reason, you need to be on the lookout for the hell-raisers as well as the gossips so that you can either get them to straighten up or sit down. The amazing truth is many of the ministries that are struggling today are struggling because they've got people standing up who should be sitting down in their churches. These people bring so much chaos into the churches that the members start leaving and finding other churches to attend. Make sure the people in your church operate in oneness, and anytime you notice an Ananias or Sapphira lurking about the congregation, be sure to remain prayerful about them and rebuke them whenever need be.

10. **Learn from the mistakes of others.** Sometimes, we notice the mistakes that other ministers make, but instead of jotting them down and learning from them, we talk about them. Utilize every negative situation for what it really is: a teachable moment. At the same time, make sure you have a teachable spirit and be willing to adhere to wise council.

Common Mistakes When Launching a Ministry

It goes without saying, there are many common mistakes people use when launching their ministries. Below are five (avoidable) common mistakes people make when launching ministries:

1. **Trying to launch the ministry too fast.** Be patient. There is a time and a

season for everything, and oftentimes, when God tells us that He is going to use us to launch ministries, He is speaking in future tense. This means you ought to prepare to launch, but don't launch a ministry hastily and end up having to shut it back down. Take your time, be prayerful, and prepare for whatever God has assigned you to do.

2. **Not praying about the people on the ministry team.** Honestly, this is probably the most common mistake made by people in leadership. After all, we're human, and the human side of us marvels at the gifts, talents, and anointings we see on others, but we can't allow ourselves to be so mesmerized by what we see that we ignore what God wants to show us. Pray about every person who applies or volunteers to be a part of the ministry's leadership team, and don't be afraid to reject people if God says they should be seated.

3. **Launching without doing the**

necessary research and paperwork.
Honestly, when God speaks to us, our spirits will oftentimes leap and we'll get so excited that we want to do whatever He told us to do hastily. But just like God told us to guard our hearts, He wants us to guard the ministries He's assigned us to. How do we do this? We do this by conducting the necessary research to find out what we need in our states and communities to legally run our ministries, and next, we need to make sure the necessary paperwork is filed so we don't leave a door open for Satan to attack our ministries.

4. **Not properly or professionally branding the ministry.** Because so many leaders are hasty and want to get everything done in their own time, they neglect to brand their ministries, and the ones who do brand, often don't brand their ministries professionally. Your branding represents your church, and your church represents God. You should never settle for less than perfect

branding, nor should you neglect to have branding for your church.

5. **Relying on the church members to keep the church's doors open.** I understand we need money to start and run churches, but please know that God won't give you an assignment, and then, neglect to give you the provision you'll need to carry out that assignment. We've just got to stop using the seed God gives us to get new suits, new cars, and fancy hairdos because when we do this, we put a burden on the people of God to keep the doors of the church open. When people are not burdened to give, they'll give more. Take whatever seed God gives you and build your ministry. As you continue to obey God with the seed, what you'll notice is you don't "need" the people to give to the church to keep the doors of the church open or the lights on. Instead, you'll have more than enough to carry out the task yourself, and when the people of God see how God is blessing the

Starting a Ministry

>ministry, they will give more. It's human nature to want to sow into whatever appears to be successful, but to withhold from whatever looks to be unsuccessful.

Starting a ministry can be easy or difficult, depending on the faith level and vision of each individual minister. If you are looking to start a ministry, make sure you are in God's will and you follow proper protocol to ensure your ministry is devil-proof. And know this: the struggles and opposition that come your way aren't powerful enough to close your ministry's doors, but the purpose of those struggles is to scare you into retreating. Don't run from your assignment. Just trust God and He will guide you from one level to the next until you've reached your assigned place.

Building a Ministry

Building your ministry isn't the same as starting a ministry. When you're building a ministry, you've already established the name of that ministry, accepted your assigned role for that ministry, and taken care of the legal stuff associated with the laws in your state. Nevertheless, building a ministry is finding your team, finding your building's location (if you will have a physical church), branding that ministry, and gathering members for the ministry. Starting a ministry is easy, but building a ministry can be challenging enough to make you question your assignment. The problem is oftentimes a person building a ministry is new to the building process, and therefore, don't understand and are not mentally prepared for the challenges associated with building a ministry. After all, when we're seeing the visions in our minds and jotting everything down on paper, it all looks so easy, but most of us weren't prepared for the "no's" we'd receive, the opposition we'd face, or the betrayals we'd endure. Truthfully, a lot of men and women of God who have established ministries failed at launching or building those ministries initially because of lack of knowledge coupled with opposition. Building a ministry isn't about jotting your ideas down on a sheet a paper; building a ministry starts with jotting God's instructions down on your heart and following them. Sometimes, we get so caught up in our own visions for our ministries that we become blinded to God's vision for the ministry He's assigned us to, meaning, we make the ministry all about us and not about Him. One of the most common mistakes is taking on the mentality that your church is a business, rather than it being a hospital for souls. When a minister sees the church as a business rather than a ministry, that minister will build his or her's business, that minister will not build a ministry. The difference is when you build a business, you will make decisions that are in the best interest of your business, but when

Building a Ministry

you build a ministry, your decisions will be based on the best interest of your members. That's the root of a lot of church hurt. So many people build "their" ministries, and they position people in "their" ministries according to their own understanding. They don't consult with God as to what those people's true titles or assignments in the kingdom are, so, for example, if brother Reggie has the Apostolic calling on his life, but joins himself to a church, the Pastor of that church may be blind to brother Reggie's assignment. Nevertheless, he will notice the anointing on brother Reggie's life, and he may seek to keep brother Reggie under his ministry because of jealousy or simply because brother Reggie has been so instrumental to the building of his church that he doesn't think his ministry will survive without brother Reggie. Now, if brother Reggie finally decided to answer the call on his life, his Pastor may find himself offended and do or say things intended to defame brother Reggie's name. Believe it or not, these behaviors have become commonplace in today's church, and this is because many churches are taking on

Building a Ministry

the traditional, religious Pharisee mentality, where the leaders call and appoint other leaders, rather than looking for the called and chosen seated amongst them.

The strength of your ministry lies in the knowledge you've acquired, your ability to hear from God, and your willingness to obey God. Some of the strongest ministries are ran by men and women who aren't intimidated by the individual anointings on the sheep they're called to pastor and the leaders who are coming up amongst them. When you can accept, for example, that brother Reggie has a greater call on his life than you have on yours, you can effectively lead brother Reggie until God releases him from under your care. Make no mistake about it. God will re-position the man once he's gotten all he needs to get from you, but this isn't a strike against you, it is the divine and perfect plan of God.

To build a ministry, you first need a building, and that is, of course, if you're called to launch a physical church. When choosing a building,

Building a Ministry

always be prayerful and don't grab the first broken building you see just because you can afford it. Oftentimes, the building itself ends up being a testimony. What God often does with leaders who entrust Him with locating the building they will have their services in is He will often lead them to buildings they can't afford. These buildings are oftentimes immaculate, and acquiring those buildings will almost always look impossible. That's because God loves to take the impossible and make them possible. How else is His name glorified? God uses every opportunity presented to Him to build your faith and encourage His people.

Before purchasing or renting out a building, ask the Lord what city and state He's assigning you to. If you build a church in a city you're not called to, your church will become nothing more than a religious establishment because of your rebellion.

After you've been instructed as to where you ought to go, be sure to remain prayerful when choosing your building. Again, don't always go for what you can afford. A lot of times, we get rejected for certain buildings, and it's not the lender who's rejecting us. It is God, through the lender, who is rejecting us because we're attempting to let fear and unbelief choose where we'll have church services, when God wants us to choose with our faith. Oftentimes, it's that building that we really want, but think we can't afford that God wants us to have. And the truth is, we cannot afford those buildings, but God can. Let God choose the building that He wants to bless His people with, and then, take the necessary steps to purchasing or renting that building.

Next, as mentioned in the previous chapter, we have to contact our local and state offices to see what permits and licenses we need for our buildings, or to obtain recognition in our states. Again, you do not need the 501c3, so if you can help it, don't place yourself under the strong arm of the government. The best thing to do is retain a lawyer to conduct the necessary research and file the necessary paperwork for you. Having a lawyer on your side makes registering and running your ministry a lot easier.

Branding Your Ministry
Branding your ministry will be as easy or as difficult as you make it out to be. One of the first things you should do is get is a website. Let's face it. We live in the age of technology, and the great thing about technology is it allows us to reach more people than we ordinarily would be able to reach. Nowadays, our church members aren't just limited to the people who sit in the buildings we preach in, but we can have members in other states and countries if we'll only stream our services online.

Having a website allows others to read more about your ministry, review videos of sermons, and make donations. At the same time, it gives them the opportunity to send in their prayer requests, and this helps us to become more effective leaders.

The next thing you'll need for branding is your

Building a Ministry

logo. Even though the website is far more important than the logo, if you can, get the logo first so you can submit it to the web designer before he or she designs the site. That way, you don't have to pay the designer again to upload the logo once you've gotten it.

Your ministry's logo is just a visual graphic that represents the ministry. Its colors, design, and imagery should all be representative of your ministry's strengths, and of course, your ministry is only as strong as your faith. So, if you have a healing and deliverance ministry, your logo would likely consist of images that represent healing and deliverance. If your ministry's strengths are all of the gifts of the Holy Spirit, your logo could either consist of several images representing the gifts of the Spirit, or you can simply showcase an empty cross on your logo. An empty cross represents the fact that Jesus lives; it represents the fulfillment of God's promise.

You'll also need brochures, business cards, videos, and many other forms of branding.

Building a Ministry

Don't rush to do everything, but, at the same time, don't procrastinate in getting done what needs to be done. When you can afford to get the necessary branding done, go ahead and start branding the ministry. When you don't have the funds, don't spend that time trying to find someone to give you what you want. Spend that time writing down what you want and petitioning to God for those things. Some of the ministries with the best brands are the ones who were branded slowly and excellently, where the leaders weren't trying to get ahead of God, but instead, waited for their finances to catch up with their visions.

Gathering Members
One of the biggest mistakes I've seen other leaders make is trying to go after people who were members of other ministries. This is not only disrespectful, but it can be costly. How so? Let's say that brother Reggie is a member of Pastor Douglas's church, and has been a member there for the last six years. Brother Reggie once struggled with violence and perversion, but every since he started going to

Building a Ministry

Pastor Douglas's church, he has been a better man. He has learned the importance of forgiveness, he's learned to walk in that forgiveness, and he has renounced sexual perversion. Now, brother Reggie is a happily married man, but one day, brother Reggie becomes offended with Pastor Douglas because Pastor Douglas rightfully rebuked him because of how he'd been treating his wife. Reggie's wife, Kim, had complained to the pastor that Reggie had been very condescending towards her, and she expressed her concerns about brother Reggie's odd relationship with the church's youth pastor. Being a shepherd, Pastor Douglas observes brother Reggie and notices that he's been spending too much time with the youth pastor, so the pastor decides to pull him to the side and rebuke him. Brother Reggie becomes offended and stops coming to church altogether.

One day, you come across brother Reggie, and he starts telling you about his argument with Pastor Douglas. You can clearly hear that

Building a Ministry

the person who is wrong is brother Reggie, but instead of rebuking him and sending him back to the man God is using to shepherd him, you decide to invite him to your church. What you didn't realize was for the last few days, the Lord had been dealing with brother Reggie's heart, and he was simply reaching out to you in hopes that you'd be honest with him, but instead, you saw an opportunity in it for you. He'd be a new member, and he'd likely bring a few people with him.

Now, brother Reggie goes to your church, and he has fully returned to the vomit that God used Pastor Douglas to lead him away from. Now, he's beating on his wife, cheating on his wife, addicted to pornography, and unrepentant. That's because you weren't the shepherd God entrusted with brother Reggie's soul, and in cases like this, the enemy uses one pastor to help lead another pastor's sheep away from him or her. The point is, you can't gather members by stealing them. Let God send the people He wants to send into your church, but in the meantime, just keep branding, preaching, and advertising.

Building a Ministry

The proper way to gather member is by being faithful with the ones you're entrusted with now. **Matthew 25:23 (KJV):** His lord said unto him, Well done, good and faithful servant; thou hast been faithful over a few things, I will make thee ruler over many things: enter thou into the joy of thy lord.

God will often send a few people your way to minister to. Most great churches started in someone's living room, and most great churches started off with fewer than five members. You take the five God has sent your way and lead them in love, teaching them the gospel of Jesus Christ, and covering them in prayer. As a shepherd, you ought to pray for your flock, feed your flock, and even fast for them. When they began growing up in the Lord, and God sees that He could trust you with more souls, He will send more. Let your church grow naturally, and don't rush to fill up the seats in your building. A lot of leaders go to great lengths to fill up their churches, only to end up dealing with a lot of scandal because they're trying to lead people they weren't chosen to lead. Seeds grow naturally, and when watered correctly, they continue to grow and blossom into whatever they are. Every person in your church is a seed, and your job is to water them. Nevertheless, there are different types of seeds in this earth, and some seeds don't grow well in certain climates. Some plants need year around sunshine, whereas, others depend on the four seasons to grow and produce life after their own. The same goes with people. Some people need to be seated in deliverance ministries, whereas, others need to be seated under teachers because they don't read their bibles like they should.

Your branding will attract many people to your church, and if you don't have a physical church building, your branding will attract many to your online presence. That's why it's important to make sure your branding is polished, you post regularly to your site, and that you regularly engage with your followers. Now, to engage doesn't mean that you get personal with them, but you should always be watchful, prayerful, and encourage them whenever you can. Additionally, make sure that you have membership forms and the answers to frequently asked questions on your website.

Below are three steps to building your ministry.
1. **Challenge the impossible:** As leaders, we always want to do what makes sense to us, but that's not always the right thing to do. It seems right to us to get what we can afford, and do whatever we think we can do in our own might, but walking in faith is something we often stray away from doing. Nevertheless, God wants to bless us with buildings we can't afford and make those things that are impossible to us possible through Him. The problem is when we are faced with a choice, we often choose what makes the most sense to us, but faith will always choose what makes no sense at all. We've got to walk by faith and not by sight. We've got to challenge the impossible by confronting it with the

Building a Ministry

Word until it becomes possible.

2. **Believe God over what you can see:** The truth is our natural man is blind to the things of the spirit, but because we're not accustomed to using our spiritual eyes, most of us don't realize we're blind. We depend on our natural vision to guide us through the earth, and because we've gotten accustomed to depending on what we can see, we tend to believe our eyes over the Word. Build your faith by studying the Word and meditating on the Word. As your faith is nourished, you will find yourself trusting God more, and it is after you've learned to trust Him that you can build and run a life changing ministry.

3. **Lead by example:** Not only will the members of the church follow the God in you, but other leaders will look to you for guidance. Some people will follow you because they don't believe what you're preaching, so they want to be around to see your fall. Some people will follow you because they're not sure what to

believe, so they want to see if the God you preach about is truly omnipotent. And then, some people will follow you because they love the Lord and want to know Him more. Every person who follows your ministry will do so for their own personal reasons, but whatever their reasons are, you need to make sure you lead by example. If you're telling people how to get the faith they'll need to move heaven, you need to demonstrate that faith. This starts off in the purchasing or building of the church. If you're getting a building you can afford, people will credit you for the building and not God. Sure, in their religiousness, they'll give God the glory verbally, but in their hearts, they will acknowledge you. Nevertheless, if you get the building you can't afford, the people have no choice but to glorify God when they witness you demonstrating your faith and getting that building. Faith is the building block of ministry; it is the overcomer of all that is

Building a Ministry

> impossible. You need to demonstrate faith in order to teach it. Lead by example and not by mere words.

Building a ministry is about taking the impossible, making it possible, and then, teaching others to do the same through Christ Jesus. It's more than just retaining a building, throwing a few banners up, and calling it a church. Anyone can do that. Building a ministry where God is glorified is about challenging the realm of possibilities with impossibilities, and then, making the impossible submit to the Word in you. It's about doing something no ordinary man or woman can do. Remember, Jezebel's false prophets prophesied and built altars, but what they could not do was get their god to prove himself because false prophets speak to false gods. Elijah called fire from heaven and proved that YAHWEH is the only true and living God.

God wants to show Himself mighty, but we often restrict Him by trying to move in our own

Building a Ministry

might, nevertheless, when building a ministry, you should always make sure that the building blocks of your ministry is faith. Faith does not appeal to the possible as much as it challenges the impossible.

Faith Versus Goliath

When David went on the battlefield to fight with Goliath, he didn't have the strength or training to overcome the giant. He didn't have any tangible weapon that appeared to be powerful enough to bring down Goliath, nevertheless, he went on the field with faith and a slingshot. I can imagine that many of the people on both sides of that confrontation thought that David was about to lose. They didn't expect such a young and scrawny boy to take down a trained warrior. Nevertheless, David went on the battlefield and took down a man that most of the Jews were afraid to challenge, a giant who had been so confident in his own abilities that he'd been taunting the Israelites.

We are all modern day versions of David, and our giants are the things that we refer to or think of as impossible. Even though there are some things that appear to be naturally and financially possible to others, those things often appear to be impossible to us. In other words, our giants are those mountains we can't seem to get over.

I can imagine that if God took 250 of today's leaders, placed them in front of Mount Everest, and told them to get to the other side of those mountains, many of the leaders would try to find their way around those mountains. Why is this? We've been conditioned to believe that shortcuts save us time and help us to get to where we want or need to be without the added effort. And while this may be somewhat true, many people don't realize that each step of our journeys is necessary to not only getting us to our assigned destinations, but processing us along the way. As we go through life, we'll endure many changes of heart and moments of deliverance. Had we found shortcuts, we would've missed out on getting the changed minds and the deliverance we needed to get us to where we were called to be. Had we taken one of the many shortcuts offered to us by the enemy, we'd probably still be lost in our sin, trying to find a creative way out. Many of us did take shortcuts, only to find ourselves chastened and rerouted back to God's will. We saw something in sin that we wanted, and we thought that the path of righteousness was the long way to whatever it was that we wanted. We took the wrong paths, and found ourselves going in the wrong direction without a clue. We tried to play God and failed.

Sure, you want to start the ministry God has given you, and you want to successfully run that ministry, but before you do this, you first need to get a better understanding of what "success" is. A lot of today's leaders have been led astray by their understandings of what success is. They think that success is having a large church full of members, an ever-growing bank account, a mansion, and a beautiful wife to call their own. So, they set out to get the things they want, rather than letting God build them up to build the ministries He's given them to launch. Because they misunderstood what success is, they went

Faith Versus Goliath

astray after their own lusts, causing many of God's people to fall. Their lives have been riddled with scandal, and their families are falling apart at the seams. Their health is failing and the devil is throwing slumber parties at their homes every night. They're going through all of this because, even though they understood they'd been called by God, they misunderstood the directions He told them to go in. They started chasing their ideas of success, and found themselves in some pretty dark places.

Success to many people means different things. Success, to a thief, is when he successfully robs another person. Success, to a murderer, is taking someone's life and getting away with it. Success, to a singer, is singing a song beautifully without getting choked up or forgetting the words. Success, to a surgeon, is when he performs surgery on his patient and the patient lives a more quality life because of it. As you can see, success varies by individual, nevertheless, success, to a minister of the gospel of Jesus Christ should only be

Faith Versus Goliath

defined by the Word of God and not redefined by the things of this world. Success, to a God-fearing leader, should always be winning souls and changing lives. When a minister of the gospel attributes success to his or her own flesh, that minister can become a danger to the body of Christ. That's why we have to ask ourselves as often as we can, "What does success mean to me?" This means we need to have a heart of God in order to be successful in our ministries.

Once you understand success, the next thing you need to do is identify your Goliath and challenge him. What's impossible to you? What is it that you want so badly that it has grown up and become a giant to you? We often run from and try to avoid every Goliath that stands in our paths, but you can't change an impossibility by avoiding it. You have to overcome it with the blood of the Lamb and the power of your testimony. You have to stand your ground and refused to be moved by fear, doubt, or unbelief. Goliath appeared to be impossible because of his large frame, big

Faith Versus Goliath

mouth, and impressive war record. David appeared to be already defeated because of his small frame and inexperience.
Nevertheless, David didn't fight Goliath in the arena of the flesh. He called on the name of the Lord, and God gave David the victory the moment David accepted the challenge. The same goes for us. We have the victory; we've just got to accept whatever challenges come our way so that God can defeat them through us.

Today, you may be starting a ministry or trying to get past the obstacles you've faced in your ministry, but I want to encourage you by telling you to face the giant and stop trying to avoid it. God is not asking you to face that giant with your own power. He wants you to face it in the power of the Word by brandishing your faith in the Word, and then, taking down every giant who dares to challenge you. It's time to stop avoiding impossibilities, and start challenging them until they become possibilities, and those possibilities turn into opportunities. Starting and running a ministry is a journey that

Faith Versus Goliath

requires a constant building of your faith, renewing of your mind, and redefining of your character. When you accept the call on your life, you are accepting the challenges that come with that call. You can't get hired by the city as a police officer and expect to choose which crimes you're most comfortable fighting against. You have to be willing to come outside your comfort zone and wrestle men who may be twice your size. That's the responsibility that comes with the badge. The same thing goes for ministry. You can't choose which devils to fight, which mountains to climb, and which sheep to pasture. You have to accept the assignment as a whole. Yes, you will be confronted by many mountains that will appear to be impossible to climb, but those are the mountains God wants to bring you over so that He gets the glory. Find your Goliath, challenge him, and bring him down. That's when you'll be elevated and find yourself going up the mountain with little to no effort. Every time you challenge and defeat a Goliath, you will find yourself on a new level of the mountain that you're climbing, and each time, the climb

Faith Versus Goliath

will become easier and the giants will begin to look smaller as your faith grows up. God takes pleasure in defeating impossibilities. We've just got to give them over to Him and let Him demonstrate His unlimited power to us and through us. My assignment for you is to jot down three giants that have intimidated you, and then, confront them. Let's finally get in a place where we can not only demonstrate the supernatural to the people in the congregation, but we can experience the supernatural power of God by taking on our Goliaths, and watching God defeat them.

Luke 1:37 (KJV): For with God nothing shall be impossible.

www.ingramcontent.com/pod-product-compliance
Lightning Source LLC
Chambersburg PA
CBHW060522100426
42743CB00009B/1407